FROM LAND GIRL TO VICAR'S WIFE

Overleaf: The poem 'Vicaress' is from Verse from the Vestry *by S.J. Forrest and is reproduced here by kind permission of the publisher Mowbray, now Continuum.*

'Vicaress' from *Verse from the Vestry* by S.J. Forrest.

The Vicarage is empty and the wardens now intend
To clarify the Bishop on the type to send
And guarantee a clergyman of dedicated life
Though personally, we'd prefer to guarantee his wife.
We'd like a proper lady who is versatile and strong,
Unlikely to monopolise the Vicar's time for long.
She mustn't be an invalid or suffer from defect
Or give her husband reason for his duty to neglect.

We need a woman competent to organise a house
With energy, efficiency, intelligence and nous,
In all the art of motherhood enabled to excel,
(With preference for one who is a gardener as well.)
She ought to be hospitable and keep an open home,
With eagerness to entertain the many who will come.
To caller and to visitor displaying furthermore,
Unhesitating promptitude in opening the door.

Nor should she make the Vicarage a stationary perch,
But move among the people in the parish and the church
And show a ready sympathy, compassionate and quick,
By visiting the lonely, the aged and the sick.
Ability to organise, and take an active lead
Is something that our candidate will obviously need.
We can't afford a curate, who involves a tidy fee,
And why a parish worker, when a clergy wife is free?

To run the Mothers' Union and supervise the flowers
Should captivate her interest and occupy the hours,
While for her idle leisure time the parish life provides
A splendid opportunity as Captain of the Guides.
And so we now consider it legitimate to claim
A Vicar with a helpmate who is worthy of the name,
For if we fail to see her in the Sunday School and Hall,
We shall not feel our Vicar is a married man at all.

From
LAND GIRL
to
Vicar's Wife

To Jacquine

Anne Fountain

Anne Fountain

EX LIBRIS PRESS

Published in 2000 by
Ex Libris Press
1 The Shambles
Bradford on Avon
Wiltshire

Printed in England by
Cromwell Press, Trowbridge

ISBN 1 903341 04 3

CONTENTS

FARINGDON

ENNERDALE

Photograph of Raymond Fountain by Lorna Proctor.

St. Luke's Hospital, Bradford, Social work Department. Anne Hall second from right.

PROLOGUE

Having left the Land Army in 1946, a one-year emergency training course run by the Institute of Almoners led to work in hospitals in Bradford, Yorkshire. After a few months work at the Royal Infirmary I was transferred to St. Luke's Hospital to start a Medical Social Work department. I was living in digs and, when I decided to try the local churches, was advised to attend Bradford Cathedral services. My Senior colleague, Dorothy Hayes, decided to accompany me. Although Dorothy was a Presbyterian, she wanted to experience an Anglican Cathedral service. We attended an impressive service for a very full congregation with a wonderful choir.

It was at this service I first set eyes on Raymond Fountain, a minor Canon who read the second lesson. I was given a premonition that he was to be my husband. Not having had such an experience and quite sure that this could not possibly be true, yet left wondering, I said to Dorothy after the service that if that clergyman had come down the aisle and proposed to me I would marry him. This had us both laughing and Dorothy said he certainly was good looking and very like the actor James Mason.

Being involved in helping with youth work at the Cathedral I saw a lot of this clergyman who was known to us all as 'Skip', being Captain of the Boys Brigade. I'd had several male friends with whom I'd enjoyed good friendships but, though Skip and I often talked over church affairs when we met, and though at times he came to the Almoner's office to join me for a cup of tea, our relationship was always very formal. Nevertheless, for the first time I was suffering the agony of falling in love. The pain intensified as there was talk about Skip leaving Bradford to take on his own church and parish.

He was about to go on holiday and was taking the short morning service which I attended most days before work. Skip stopped me as I was leaving church and asked me, "Can you come down?"

Assuming he had some work for me to do, perhaps with the Youth Fellowship during his absence, I said, "Yes, I can came down," thinking he wanted to see me in the Clergy House.

"Catch the 3.18 from Victoria and I'll meet you at Pulborough station," Raymond called back to me as the Provost was calling to him to hurry if he wanted a lift to the station.

Peggy Dunn, a schoolteacher friend, was leaving the church with me and told me Raymond was just off on two weeks holiday. I stood outside the Cathedral wondering what on earth Raymond meant. It struck me he must have written to me at my digs and I had stayed two nights at the Vicarage. I shot back to my digs and discovered that I had accepted an invitation to his Sussex home for the weekend. I hadn't his address so felt I must go to Pulborough.

Mother was annoyed when I rang home to say I was not coming to them for the Bank Holiday weekend as I was going to Sussex. She assumed I was going to get engaged as such a gentleman would not invite a woman to his home unless intending to get engaged, yet I had not told her. Raymond's mother also assumed we were getting engaged since she gave Raymond a family diamond ring she felt sure he'd need that weekend. Certainly we had not thought of this, Raymond intending we get to know each other without the Parish getting ideas about any outings we might have together. After delightful downland walks I had to admit to Raymond that I was sad he was leaving Bradford and I would miss him as all the congregation would; Raymond then managed to say he was hoping he could take me with him.

Raymond's parents were greatly relieved to hear the news as they had assumed we would tell them of our engagement on our arrival, and had been so worried that perhaps we were not, after all, getting engaged. They said they had both taken aspirin after sleepless nights!

While Raymond hastened to telephone the Provost, I rang up Dorothy Hayes, and she at once remembered the service when I first saw Raymond and decided I would like to marry him.

Bradford Cathedral personalities, from left to right: The Very Rev. John Tiarks, Provost; Bishop Blunt, Bishop of Bradford Diocese; Raymond Fountain, Succentor and Bishop's Chaplain; The Revd. Donald Coggan, Principal of Divinity, later Bishop of Bradford.

Wedding group outside Bradford Cathedral

PROLOGUE

Walking up the long aisle of Bradford Cathedral on 17th November 1951 on the arm of cousin John Hall, I was rather overawed to find a thousand or more congregation packing the church, but what a great send-off. The service, taken by the Provost, was wonderful, as the full choir had turned out to see Raymond married and they sang their hearts out. It was a lovely service, and the Boys Brigade formed a guard of honour as we left the Cathedral, having had the Blessing of Bishop Blunt.

After the reception in the Cathedral Hall, gate-crashed by many choir and Boys Brigade, John Tiarks drove us to the Vicarage to change, and then on to Leeds to catch a London train. As we passed the Cathedral Hall the Boy's Brigade were going to the station with band instruments. They intended to see us off, and were sad to find only Raymond's relatives leaving from Bradford. The relatives enjoyed the cheerful band send-off, and one young man gave Mrs. Fountain a copy of *Woman and Home* intended for Raymond as a present from the Boys Brigade.

Sad though we were at severing our link with those good Bradford friends, we were ready for the peace and joy of a quiet two weeks in Cornwall, while my good sisters and Mother undertook to see the furniture moved into Hildenborough Vicarage and to do what they could to have it ready for our return. We were extremely grateful to have the break before putting in an appearance in Hildenborough.

It was good to have my mother and sisters at Hildenborough to greet us, and to find how well they had it all arranged, with much unpacking already completed. We were sad my sisters had to get back to their work before Raymond's Induction on 11th December, but they said they would be back to see more of Hildenborough at the first opportunity.

In those few days before the Induction we had many visits from parishioners to bid us welcome and to introduce themselves, and I was slowly waking up to the fact that I was a Vicar's wife and much was now to be expected of me. I felt very little confidence in my ability to make much of a success in such a rôle.

HILDENBOROUGH

St. John the Evangelist, Hildenborough

Our First Parish

I was the last to dash across to the church that evening, having first seen family and friends out. Thankfully I found a free seat, only to be told by an elderly churchwarden,

"I'm sorry, that seat is reserved for the Vicar's wife."

With relief I owned up to being that person, and with apologies he withdrew hastily as the choir of men and boys emerged from the vestry, leading in procession, the Reverend Russell White, Vicar of Tonbridge, patron of the parish, walking with Raymond, Vicar elect. They were followed by the Archdeacon and the churchwardens, carrying their wands of office. Following them was the chaplain to the Bishop of Rochester, Christopher Chavasse, carrying the Bishop's pastoral staff in front of the Bishop. The Bishop was formally bowed into his chair on the chancel step facing the congregation and the wardens then led the Archdeacon, the Patron (representing the Simeon Trustees) and the Vicar-elect locked out of the south-west door, to knock to gain admission. Once inside he had to ring the church bell. (Members of the congregation liked to count the strokes on the bell, thinking they might be some indication of how long the Vicar would stay.)

The procession then moved on as choir and congregation sang the Hymn 'We love the place O God, wherein Thine honour dwells', pausing at font, lectern, pulpit and altar, as each appropriate verse had been sung. The Vicar was then led by the Archdeacon who 'caused the Vicar to be seated' in his chair in the choir. The Vicar having promised to carry out a Vicar's duties faithfully, and to obey his Bishop; he was then able to read the week's notices as indication that he had now been inducted to the living and Vicarage.

All the duties Raymond was required to promise to do seemed to be quite awe-inspiring. The Bishop gave him a great welcome in his sermon and preached on St. John the Baptist's preparing of the way for the coming of Christ, urging the congregation to support their new Vicar in their prayers.

Escorting Raymond's parents to the village hall to receive the official welcome, my thoughts turned to my early youth, when I held clergy in great awe, as having had a very special call to work for God. I was sometimes ragged about suffering from 'Parsonitis'. Now I was to be involved in this great work. In Bradford, when Raymond had introduced me to Bishop Blunt, to whom he was then chaplain, Bishop Blunt did not paint a very rosy picture of the rôle of Vicar's wife. He looked at me rather sorrowfully, saying,

"You are taking on a very demanding life as wife to a Vicar. There will be little time for recreation with such involvement in parish work. You will have a very busy husband with most of his time taken up with the church family, and very small income, which can be a problem and a worry. However, with God's help it can be very rewarding in many ways."

I had already experienced having to make an appointment to see Raymond during our brief engagement, in order to make the necessary wedding arrangements. Raymond was to be single-handedly in charge of this church, and I was already becoming aware of the amount of work he would be expected to cope with, yet I felt gratitude to God for giving me this privileged life, helping Raymond.

We found the Village Hall very crowded but, having secured seats for Mr. and Mrs. Fountain, I approached a lady pouring teas in the hope of getting a quick one to them, as they were elderly and tired after the journey from Sussex and the long service. I was told, somewhat brusquely, if I would just go and sit down the teas would be brought round, but the churchwarden came and asked me to join Raymond on the platform to receive the speech of welcome. We were told the Bishop regretted having to leave as soon as the service was over, as he had to take a funeral the next day in Rochester. Some young Naval cadets, marching back to camp in the dark, had been killed in a dreadful road accident. He would have to prepare for this service which he did not look forward to taking.

On leaving the platform I received an apology for not having been recognised and for not being given the teas. After a brief chat and a laugh together, I joined Raymond at the door, meeting parishioners as they were leaving the hall.

Mr. Hendry had been Vicar's warden for a good many years and, now in his nineties, knew most villagers and a lot about the parish, and was looking forward to having a talk with Raymond. He and Mr. Crick said they would like a chat with Raymond on Monday morning.

Mr. Crick had recently become people's warden; during the interregnum the last people's warden died of a heart attack very suddenly at the farewell gathering when Mr. Fraser, the previous Vicar, was leaving and was being presented with a parting present. A dreadful shock for all those present.

On returning to the Vicarage, I saw Raymond's parents settled for the night and, though there was a lot of unpacking still to do, my Mother and sisters had done wonderfully well, finding all the immediate essentials for us. I thankfully went up to bed, leaving Raymond to prepare for Sunday services. He was still trying to unpack more books, and I was sure he was going to be pretty late getting to bed, but it was not a job with which I could be of much help. I was sorry not to have met the Bishop as Raymond knew him well from college days at St. Peter's, Oxford, when the Bishop had been Principal of the college.

Hildenborough Church had been built in 1844 at a time when there was a desire for more churches in villages, rather than worshippers having to travel long distances to the nearest parish church. There had been nine, well loved Vicars before Raymond, and Mr. Fraser was especially well-loved, having seen the parish through the difficult war years.

Mr. Fraser seemed to have had a good private income, since there was some concern felt by the Church Council at having to find a salary for Raymond, as Mr. Fraser had apparently had merely his expenses paid by the church. I was told he and his wife had had paid help in the house and garden, leaving them fairly free for parish visiting. As it was a large Vicarage set in three acres of ground, we could appreciate the need for this help. We were glad to keep their gardener to help us once a week. Mr. Fermer had a brother who worked in the churchyard though he suffered with arthritis.

Above and below: Hildenborough Vicarage.

Left: Raymond and Anne Fountain at the Hildenborough church gate.

(Raymond thought of our gardener as 'terra firma' and his brother as 'in firma' to differentiate between the two Mr. Fermers.) The ground floor of the Vicarage had a large living room with French windows opening out into a garden with a vast lawn and equally big kitchen garden. A very large dining room had a long, wide mahogany dining table. A centre passage from front door through garden doors divided off the kitchen which was entered by a short passage and had cupboards either side. The big square kitchen/breakfast room had a stone floor; there were cupboards built round the three walls, an old coke boiler and oven alongside next to the door into the small scullery. On the first floor were four, large bedrooms, a bathroom and dressing room. A door half-way up the stairs led to three attic rooms, one a tank room and one full of Vicarage garden party clutter and large Victorian family Bibles, presumably presented to previous Vicars or to the church.

When I had my first look at the Vicarage with Mother she was quite horrified when she saw the scullery. There was an old pump by the side of an old-fashioned brown (earthenware?) sink, but alongside was a rather more modern deep sink and old-fashioned taps. Two steps behind was a gas stove and a flight of worn stone steps led to very roomy cellars. (Raymond was not long in fixing a board over the steps and railing it round.) The back door ran up over a sloping stone floor, so was worn away in the corner, which a certain rat found convenient when wishing to visit the pantry.

In the breakfast room was a row of bells, ascending a scale and giving different tones, which told of the days of servants in the attics. The dilapidated wallpaper on the stairs went up far too great a height for us to do any redecorating, and apart from sweeping away cobwebs, the walls remained much the same during our stay.

Knowing how little domestic work I had done, having spent war years farming, then living in digs while doing hospital social work, mother couldn't imagine how I would run this establishment and I soon discovered it was a challenge. Rather different from my days of sitting in my office, calling in my secretary for letters having my morning coffee and afternoon tea brought to me, attending hospital management committees, doing ward rounds with consultants and occasionally being driven with them to other hospitals.

When busy in the kitchen one morning and hearing Raymond returning in the car, I was surprised by a lady poking her head round the back door,

"Oh, Mrs. Fountain, I see the Village Hall is booked by the church this evening, are we to tip tap?"

As I tried to think what on earth was going on in the hall, Raymond came in and asked her,

"What do we usually tip Tapp?"

Hasty withdrawal of Anne feeling rather daft.

I soon realised, however, that large rooms are easier to clean and tidy than small overcrowded rooms where one is forever moving furniture to clean round.

Lots of kind parishioners were very ready to advise on how to get the best out of ration books to good advantage when having to provide meals for the two of us and for all the entertaining that we would find Vicarage life entailed.

During our first week the unpacking of tea chests and cases still took up a lot of time, but I had plenty of breaks from this tedium, as I had many visits from church members calling to bid us welcome. Many came with lovely flowers or little gifts for the home. Most had time to stay for coffee and a chat, so I soon got to know some familiar faces, and one said I couldn't forget her name if I remembered the smallest county, Rutland. Even so it was a year or more before I discovered she had the title of 'The Honourable'. She became a great friend and was ever ready to lend a hand in the Vicarage, any ironing of Vicar's surplices, or any shopping. We only learned of her title when she told us her brother was given a place in Westminster Abbey for the Queen's Coronation.

Not being much of a socialiser, having spent war years mostly with animals, it was a real worry for me to know how one dressed for cocktail parties and evening dinner events. Mine was not an exciting wardrobe, in fact a pretty sober one.

I scarcely saw Raymond in our first week, he was so busy visiting members of the PCC (Parsh Church Council) and others helping in church work, the sick and aged and housebound who had missed the Vicar's visits during the interregnum.

In our second week we tried to get into a bit of a routine. I usually managed to go with Raymond into church for Morning Prayer, as it was generally only a fifteen-minute service taken on our own. After a rushed breakfast Raymond would spend time in the study, reading a quite considerable morning mail, and planning the necessary visits. The post often led to time-consuming tasks, such as searching the parish records for people trying to trace their ancestry, or taking flowers that had arrived by post to put on a family grave. Finding the grave from records in the church also used valuable time. Sometimes ashes of the deceased arrived by post, to await burial arrangements, and these would be kept in the church. I had not before thought much about how a Vicar spent his week, only seeing him on Sundays for the most part. Very quickly I was to learn there were never enough hours in the day to get through all the work expected of him.

We liked to spend time together each evening to pray over the day's activities and people's requests for help of one sort and another. If Raymond had evening meetings we would do Bible reading when he came to bed. After a non-stop day I was often guilty of being fast asleep while Raymond was doing the Bible reading for the day.

It was sometimes the only part of the day to enjoy togetherness.

Early Learning

The three acres of ground surrounding the Vicarage were a challenge but a church member asked if he could have the use of the kitchen garden as an allotment, while we were in Hildenborough. We were happy for him to take this over, when 'Terra Ferma' retired. It proved a great help; we were given free vegetables grown in the garden and, when he erected a hen run, we were also supplied with eggs. Not being able to cope with an orchard at the bottom of the vegetable garden, a next door neighbour was happy to care for that; he also harvested the walnuts from the tree by the orchard and saw that we had plenty of those. A riding school asked if they might rent the Vicarage field below the graveyard, so we were left only with the large lawn, a hedge and a front garden bed. The lawn was not too easy before we could afford a motor mower. It took Raymond four hours to mow the back lawn.

We were kept very busy with callers and with visiting. If the Vicar was seen gardening, it was thought that was why someone didn't get visited. If the garden was neglected, and appeared not as it once did, the Vicar was lazy. To many, the Vicar's job was thought to be cushy, having to work just on Sundays, but the church members knew that to be on call for the thousands in the parish was a full-time job, which often meant no day off in the week.

Raymond had a pretty miserable time each summer as he suffered from severe hay fever. Doctor Davison, the village doctor, arranged for him to visit a London hospital for treatment. Having had a series of tests he proved allergic to a good many flowers, dust and other things so was put on a course of injections each summer for a year or two. It did not cure the trouble, but eased it considerably, so he was not in dark glasses and busy with his handkerchief through visits and services, and at the annual garden parties.

From our first arrival on the scene, we received many an invitation to coffee or tea or to evening meals. Dr. Stanley and Kathleen Davison were very hospitable and we were invited to spend evenings at their home when Stanley and Raymond both had a free evening. Sometimes we had a restful evening listening to classical music, hearing some of their son Murray's collection of records.

I remember an amusing evening when one of the gardeners, Len Wright, and Phyllis his wife, invited us in to watch a programme they much enjoyed called 'Panorama'. What they did not know that evening, was that the chosen subject under discussion was mainly about 'women's breasts'. This caused them some embarrassment as they assured us that this was not at all like the usual subjects discussed in 'Panorama'. They would not have invited the Vicar in that evening if they had known this was to be the subject. We got them laughing with us at the way the evening turned out, and they were good friends for many years.

When Sir Arthur and Lady Page invited us in for cocktails I had no idea what I should wear, but quickly found I had no need to worry when one of the first guests to arrive after us, Mrs. Finzi warned us all not to come too close as she had just fed the pigs and had not had time to change. It gave me a lovely opening to chat to her about my pig management days and how I loved pigs.

When invited to an informal meal by Lady McFadyen and her husband, we felt relieved it was not to be too formal as we didn't go in for evening dress. We were to be their only guests. We were glad to dress informally as Raymond had no dinner jacket and I had no long evening dress, that is, until we arrived to find our host and hostess coming out to greet us, both in evening dress. However the warmth of welcome made us feel quite relaxed though, as with most of the homes we had been invited to, the meal was served by the family butler, so had a rather formal feel. Once more Land Army experience was a help to me as Lady McFadyen had a superb herd of pedigree Aberdeen Angus cattle. Hearing I had worked with one of the best pedigree shorthorn herds, I was invited to visit again to see her beautiful herd. That I really enjoyed.

The parish were now becoming interested in finding the right work for the Vicar's wife. I was asked if I would take charge of the Flower Guild. Never having had experience of flower arranging and as they had an excellent leader in Mrs. Roper, who was an artist in this work, I was happy to leave it in Mrs. Roper's hands. When invited to be President of the women's branch of the British Legion, having no knowledge of their work, and having only once had a year or two in the Territorial Army after the war, I felt I had to decline that honour, also. When invited to be Enrolling Member of the Mother's Union, though knowing nothing of their work, I felt it was expected of Vicar's wives to take on this office, so I agreed to be enrolled after some tuition from the local Presiding member, Mrs. Attlee (sister-in-law of Prime Minister Clement Attlee) and was enrolled by Raymond at a special service.

The work I felt most able to tackle was to try to interest young members of the church in forming a Youth Fellowship. Few young people were seen at services, though a good many had been confirmed in the last few years. There were few young people attending services regularly, apart from young men and boys in the church choir, trained by Mr. Stonely the organist. I did however notice one young lady, Ann Cowell, regularly attended the early service. Ann told me that there were plenty of young people in the parish, most of whom had been confirmed, but were not often seen in church. This gave us the idea of writing to those listed in the confirmation register in the last few years. Raymond wrote to ask if any would be interested in forming a Youth Fellowship at the church. Some of the letters went abroad, to let us know they had left England, but we had replies from thirty or more who were interested in the idea. A meeting was arranged to be held in the Vicarage, after Evensong.

The young men in the choir attended and about twenty-five others, which we found encouraging, until they heard we were not thinking in terms of a sports evening of darts, table tennis and the like, for which there was already provision in the village hall. We explained the idea was to help their spiritual development with religious discussions. Three choir members and two or three girls did turn up, however, which was helped by Anne Cowell trying to influence others to give the meetings a trial. This nucleus was enthusiastic, and its members attended Evensong after meeting for some weeks. Then, as the Easter holidays were upon us, we received great and unexpected help. We woke up one morning to find three tents had mushroomed on our back lawn during the night. Not too happy about this I sent Raymond to investigate. To our joy we found they were Bradford Cathedral young people.

Irvin Wilson, a keen Christian member of the Bradford Cathedral Boys' Brigade, had taken seriously the invitation Raymond had given at our wedding reception, that we would welcome any who wished to visit us in Hildenborough. He had brought along six friends from the Youth Fellowship. They were delighted to have hitchhiked all the way from Bradford Having arrived in the early hours, they pitched tents rather than disturb us. They planned to move on into France after the Bank Holiday.

Despite their short night they attended church and met some of the choir members – Brian Ash, Brian Wills and John Carter. Brian Ash told them of a hike planned for Monday and invited them along to see the lovely Kentish country. After a day with Hildenborough Youth they asked them to come back to the Vicarage for the evening.

Never having met such an amusing and lively lot of Yorkshire youngsters we had quite an invasion of young newcomers with them for the evening. After cups of tea and biscuits the Yorkshire friends treated them to Yorkshire songs in amusing dialect. When asked if all Yorkshire people were as lively and amusing (some thought of Northerners as rather a sober lot), Irvin told them of the difference it made when one became a Christian. All six gave a testimony as to how their lives had been changed. This made a great impression on our young people and numbers at the Youth Fellowship grew overnight. After this surprise visit, Irvin often visited with others from Bradford and always got a great reception and encouraged the continued attendance at Evensong before the Youth meetings.

One of the newcomers to the Youth Fellowship, Mary Hutton, who joined with her sister Susan, agreed to help me to write little 'playlets' to introduce subjects for the Sunday evening discussions. These were on the subject mainly of how we should behave as Christians, and how this should affect our decisions in life. One example being 'Should a Christian marry a non-Christian'. A few members would read from the stage a discussion supposedly between school attenders. Mary was excellent in transposing my ideas into the up-to-date school jargon. Each little discussion would end with someone going off the stage saying they didn't know what to do. The Youth Fellowship then settled in little groups to decide what advice should be given. Often very conflicting advice would be offered at which point the Vicar would be asked for his answer. They were encouraged to consult their Bibles on many issues, Raymond giving them references to look up.

Above: Youth Fellowship weekend in the Vicarage.

Right: Raymond with Irvin Wilson who brought young people to Hildenborough to help start our Youth Fellowship.

The Fellowship deepened and numbers grew. We had visits from Reg Sanger, Church Army Captain, who was Diocesan Youth Leader. Reg persuaded us to have an annual weekend conference, with the young people spending Friday and Saturday nights in the Vicarage. Each year we had twenty or more coming with their sleeping bags or camp beds – some in the attics, some in the dining room and some on the landing. Reg was given a bedroom and the conference was held in the sitting room, a book stall in the hall, the kitchen filled with hall tables and chairs and the catering done by the young people. The girls did the Sunday lunch and the boys raided the local fish and chip shop when it was their turn on Saturday. There were plenty of fun and games around bedtime, but the talks by Reg helped many into a Faith. (One of those members is now a Priest and curate at St. John the Evangelist Church in Hildenborough.)

Though well supported, a service at 9.30am on Sundays which attracted parents with young children, was discontinued. Raymond found impossible to find teaching that was suitable for adults, toddlers and children with ages ranging from ten years to teens. As there were now sufficient young people willing to help in the Sunday School, the classes could be divided to suit all age groups. Training young teachers was also a way of helping them to know how to use their Bibles in teaching, as they got used to referring to the passages being taught.

Many families continued to attend monthly Scout and Guide parades. To encourage more boys in the village to join the church, Raymond obtained film about Boys' Brigade activities, in the hope of starting a company. Men were at once attracted to the organisation and volunteered to train as officers. More films were shown at enrolment evening, encouraging many boys to enrol and this was a great encouragement. Hildenborough felt honoured when the President of the Boys Brigade, Major General Wilson-Haffenden, accepted an invitation to enrol the new Hildenborough Company.

Raymond knew the value of the Boys Brigade, having been Captain of Bradford Cathedral Company and having known many young men who became Christians through the Sunday afternoon compulsory group Bible studies. If seen to give up attending the Bible Class, they would be required to leave the Company, so few did that as the sports – swimming, soccer and band instruction were too good to lose. The military-like discipline was also effective in teaching respect for elders and officers. Tonbridge Boys' Brigade came to the enrolment, and later were to provide competition in sport and other competitions.

Major General Wilson Haffenden takes the salute at the first Parade of Hildenborough Boys Brigade who were accompanied by Tonbridge Boys Brigade.

I had been somewhat nervous at the thought of entertaining a famous Major-General, but needn't have worried. 'Haffi', as we were told to call him, was a delightful guest, and he visited us on several occasions. We noted he took the platform with Billy Graham at the Haringey Revival Rallies. More interesting to us were his tales of his time as a member of General Montgomery's staff in North Africa. He said one of his habits was to watch officers planning a campaign, and then he would make them think it out again, saying,

"Gentlemen, just what is your object?" This always got them

having a hard think, and often changed their plans.

I always left a tea making facilities in Haffi's bedroom, having once heard him making tea at 4am. I asked if he had had a restless night (we had kept him talking until very late).

"I had a wonderful night thank you, but I like a cup of tea at 4am. because I like to spend an hour in prayer early morning.

I always remember the first Sunday parade by the newly formed Boys' Brigade. The Scouts and Guides having marched up the aisle and presented their colours to the clergy in the sanctuary, in came the Boys Brigade colours very impressively carried in slow march; the boys then smartly marched in. They had quickly learnt the military style. (Sadly after we left, the next Vicar did not approve of the military style and disbanded the BB. However the boys were accepted into the Tonbridge Company, as they so enjoyed the activities.)

People and Pets

As Enrolling Member of the Mother's Union, I made a great many good friends, but I never enjoyed being a platform person, though not quite sure how to get out of it. I really put my foot in it when there was a discussion going on about whether the name 'Mother's Union' should be changed. Having met many young women in the parish not willing to join the M.U. because their divorce meant they could only become associate members, I was all for a change of name and attitude to divorce. This did not go down well, so after a somewhat unhappy meeting, I asked Mrs. Proctor, the wife of the then People's warden, if she would like to take it over, as she had been a member a long time, and would be readily accepted and very experienced at taking the Chair. Mrs. Proctor readily agreed to this and this proved popular with our branch. I was then able to spend more time getting to know the members rather better for not being on the platform.

Though not overactive in parish affairs I was kept well occupied in the Vicarage. The phone rang constantly, with messages to write out for Raymond; rooms had to be prepared for meetings, much shopping and cooking had to be done for clergy coming to preach and needing lunches before leaving, forms had be handed out for marriages or baptisms, and of course people dropped in for coffee most days. Quite a number of tramps visited in search of a meal; none went away hungry though I never offered money. Though I was aware I was criticised for not doing more in the parish, there were others who appreciated often being able to find me to hear their worries or simply to have a chat.

Most days Raymond was out more often than he was in. Sometimes I was able to go visiting with him. Towards day's end there were generally meetings he had to attend, or meetings in the Vicarage, or confirmation classes, or classes going through the Sunday lessons for young Sunday School teachers, or marriage or Baptism classes; we also had Bible study groups and prayer groups which I attended too. I was not alone however; when Raymond was out and about, I had a magnificent cat companion 'Nuts', so called because he loved to chase nuts. He was a large, long-coated, black and white male, very useful for rat-catching after I had once pulled out what I thought was a duster from a scullery drawer to find I had in fact pulled out an old rat. He was quickly dropped and ran under pantry cupboards. Poor rat was found dead a day or two later, Nuts having kept a quiet watch on those cupboards.

A companion was soon found for Nuts as a parishioner, Philippa Craig, came to ask if we would like a Border Collie sheepdog pup as her bitch had just had a litter. The pup was called Jimp, and having a long black and white coat made a good match for Nuts, and they became very good friends.   They would both accompany us in the evening if we took a turn in the field at the bottom of the garden, and Nuts showed no fear of any dog we might meet; in fact the dogs were usually the more wary.

Jimp was so easily trained I felt she must have learnt a lot from a working mum while in her womb. Her instant obedience when whistled was remarkable. Putting up a young deer in Knole park when still a pup, I whistled her and, to my amazement she stopped in her tracks and at once returned. She was a real delight and was soon attending church with me. She would lie quietly under my pew all the service, and few knew she was with me until we left church. One day she gate-crashed a wedding: as Raymond was giving a short talk to the couple in the chancel, in walked Jimp from the open vestry door. After having a quick look at the couple she lay at Raymond's feet. The bride was delighted because her mother ran a dog kennels, and she had grown up with dogs and thought it fitting that one should share their great moment.

Jimp was very distressed when, one morning, she heard Raymond going off in the car without her. She tore round the house looking for a way out and, finding no other way, jumped from a bedroom window on to a slight sill, landed safely in the garden, and raced to a car at the gate. The car door being open, in she got and jumped into the back seat. The driver did not see her and drove off to Tonbridge. She was offended when he sounded the horn. She always protested at that. The driver being tapped on the shoulder was most alarmed, thinking it was a gun in his back. His relief was great seeing the dog through his mirror. Having found her address on her collar, he drove her back to us, saying what a lovely character she was.

It was a heartbreak for me when a Doctor member of the church told me, as he left church after the early service, that he had seen a large black and white cat dead on the roadside as he came to church and was pretty sure it was our Nuts. He said he would bury him in his garden so that the Vicar would not see him, as it would be upsetting on his busy day. I hoped and prayed Nuts would turn up, but by evening when I told Raymond we realised it was indeed our Nuts. Raymond, Jimp and I all felt the loss keenly and we rang the RSPCA requesting another cat when they had one needing a home.

Returning to the Vicarage a few days later, we found a note on the front door mat, 'Cat in belfry'. A lively, affectionate black female, she was of course named 'Bats'. Jimp took to her at once and I found her a great companion, following me wherever I went, indoors or out. Sadly, after some months, a church member, waiting for a bus outside the Vicarage, saw Bats set off across the road, and a lad in a van deliberately accelerated and killed her outright. A boy at the bus stop picked up her body and laid it in the Convent grounds opposite and Bats was buried by Raymond in the churchyard. Erica Rutland gave us a kitten, which her pure-bred Siamese cat had rejected because he was black and white. Goofey was a survivor and lived fourteen years. He and Jimp were great pals, Goofey having been brought up by Erica's terrier when abandoned by Mum.

One evening when Raymond started a service with 'Let everything that hath breath, praise the Lord,' a perfectly timed loud Siamese meiow had us all convulsed with laughter. He seemed sensitive to the ethos of the Vicarage when I found him pulling one of Raymond's books out of the bookcase. As I rebuked him and replaced it, I read the title, *How can I find God*. Sadly, I felt unable to help.

Reaching Out

Soon after our arrival, Raymond had written to members of the church electoral roll inviting all to a meeting in the village hall. He hoped to hear views about what was expected of the church, and whether there were those who would like to do house-to-house visiting, in pairs, to welcome newcomers, and to let others know about church activities.

The response to the invitation was encouraging, and quite a large crowd arrived at the hall. As they entered, each was given a card with AD written on the top half, and BC on the lower half. The cards were in different colours, and those arriving in groups received different coloured cards. After Raymond's introductory talk all were formed into little discussion groups, all those with the same coloured cards in the same group. This divided up friends and enabled all to get to know each other. Lively discussions brought out lots of ideas, and some were interested in the idea of door-to-door visiting. These were asked to write their names and addresses on the cards under the heading, AD (Action Department). Those with an interest in Bible study and prayer groups were to sign the BC (Bible Class) section. Some volunteered for both. It was a very enjoyable evening and there seemed a very lively interest in helping with church affairs.

To help both groups we invited volunteers to a coffee evening in the Vicarage and it was arranged for church visitors of a nearby parish to give a talk on parish visiting and to tell of their experiences. Being keen evangelists these ladies related how greatly their faith was strengthened by helping others as they made these regular visits, as well as encouraging others into church life. Their faith and their talk so inspired all those at this meeting they set to work visiting with great enthusiasm and their visits were rewarded by introducing many into church attendance.

Sadly, the invitations sent out inviting people to the village hall meeting, upset one gentleman, Mr. Dean, because it was addressed to Mr. and Mrs. Dean. Mrs. Dean had died during the past interregnum and the church electoral roll had not been amended. Raymond had a letter from Mr. Dean saying how greatly this had hurt him, and he now wished never to meet Raymond. We were told Mr. Dean was an agnostic and not a church attender. Raymond sent him an apology, but we never met Mr. Dean while we were in Hildenborough.

We knew Mr. Dean's neighbour, Ian Haley, who ran a riding school in Riding Lane and Ian tried to persuade Mr. Dean to meet us without success. Ian became a very alive Christian through talks with a missionary having rides from his stable for a time, and helped many of our young folk to find a faith. Mr. Dean told him he was just going through a middle-aged crisis with his sudden interest in religion and the church. We were not the only ones to note Ian's sudden absence from church. His new-found faith had been encouraging to many church members, who now missed his attendance.

After some weeks, as we were driving along Riding Lane quite late one evening, we caught sight of Ian in his stable yard. Raymond drove in to have a chat. Ian was in a lot of pain with his knee and told us how he was treating it with horse liniment. Raymond got on to the subject of his absence from church. Ian said he had lost faith as he felt Mr. Dean was right: it was just a mid-life phase that had now passed. This led to a long and impassioned talk with Raymond. I was rather concerned about Ian's obvious pain in his leg while standing talking under the light of the moon. Raymond really laced into him about the effect he would have on the young people he had encouraged in faith by his recent testimonies, and asked if he really did believe he now knew so much better than all the great saints down the ages; were they all mistaken, and Ian Haley was so much wiser than them?

I was getting quite embarrassed and sad to see Ian looking dismayed at this onslaught, because he was very fond of Raymond and had a great respect for him. I thought I was witnessing the end of a rather wonderful friendship we enjoyed with Ian. He had spent so much time dropping in on us and sometimes discussed the Faith so enthusiastically that he kept us up until the early hours, and we delighted in these visits.

I wandered off to the pig units near the stables, and took comfort watching a sow grunting contentedly while feeding her young piglets. Ian sensed my mood and came across to assure me he was really impressed with Raymond's concern and must think it out again. Ian came to see Raymond shortly afterwards and asked if he would take him through Confirmation preparation. Although he had been confirmed at school he had not been to Communion services since his First Communion when first confirmed. Ian actually did attend Communion on a Sunday that happened to be our last Sunday in Hildenborough, to the great joy of all those attending. Very soon after we had left Hildenborough we had a sad letter from Ian's wife Jo, to say Ian had had his leg amputated and was now dying of lung cancer.

Before he died Raymond sent him a book written by Frank Drake about spiritual healing. Frank Drake had been Ian and Raymond's housemaster at their respective schools, first at Ian's and then at Raymond's. Frank was at a church in Guernsey but, hearing from us about Ian's illness, flew over and was able to minister to Ian very shortly before he died, to Ian's great joy. Jo wrote to tell us that there was a wonderful atmosphere during the service taken at Ian's bedside, and he was so pleased flowers from us had arrived that day and said he was conscious of our prayers with them.

Raymond and I went to Eastbourne for Raymond to take the funeral service in the crematorium. Who should we meet there amongst many good friends but Mr. Dean. He came to thank Raymond for a most helpful service and sermon and begged forgiveness for being 'an obstinate old fool' for having refused to meet Raymond when he was Vicar. He now greatly regretted it. Mr. Dean then became a friend with whom we kept in touch as he married Ian's sister shortly afterwards. We felt Ian had at last achieved the reconciliation he so much wanted.

Summer Events

Each year the end of June was the time for Hildenborough to hold the church garden party and sale. Mr. Cleaton-Davies, who was now Churchwarden, and his wife Gladys put a lot of effort into this event which drew crowds every year from the surrounding district. Mrs. C-D devoted most of her year to planning and organising a sale with a different look each June.

Looking ahead to this important event I decided it could be a good time to give the church a spring clean, as often it attracted visits from those attending the sale. My thoughts were interrupted by the approach of an elderly parishioner exclaiming,

"My dear. Why so serious. You know as Mother of the parish we expect you to greet us all with a smile. Though you may not know us all, we do all know you."

I apologised laughingly, explaining that my mind was miles away, thinking of all the work of the forthcoming sale. I did however try to wander round the village smiling happily at all I met until I one day overheard a couple passing saying,

"Who is that? do you know her?"

"No, I thought she must know you."

"No, maybe she's a bit balmy, poor lass."

My smiles became rather more tentative after that.

We had a church cleaner, but she was no longer young and would not want to do a spring clean alone. I found several ladies enthusiastic to help. While some polished and dusted pews and furniture in the sanctuary, others gave the red tiles in the aisle a good scrub and polish. Wearing an old pullover and slacks, I was backing out on my knees and collided with Mr. Barns, the Verger, who had come to see what was going on.

"Why you, Mrs. Fountain!" he exclaimed in shocked tones.

Was it a shock to see the Vicar's wife clad in old trousers and pullover, and scrubbing on hands and knees? I hastened to explain that we were doing a spring clean to help the cleaner and to have the church looking nice for any visitors who might look round when coming to the garden party. He retreated, pleased with our idea and agreed it would be helpful to the cleaner to have this work done.

Sadly the cleaner was not so pleased. The shock of seeing well polished red tiles down the centre aisle, instead of the usual muddy grey looking tiles, really upset her. Raymond received a letter expressing her great annoyance at this trespass, saying the Bishop had told her not to polish the tiles as it could make them dangerous. (The Bishop had an artificial leg following a disastrous boating accident just after being made Bishop; maybe he had encountered difficulty with highly polished church floors.)

A visit to the cleaner by the Vicar to explain that the clean up was intended to be a help to her, as she worked hard at it all the year. This cheered her and put matters right, but not long after she resigned and volunteers took over the work.

We were rather pleased that the Archdeacon chose that time to come and inspect the church, and was satisfied that it was being looked after. However, he did somewhat cheekily ask when we intended returning two unusual sanctuary brass lamps to the Mecca café. They each had three brass balls like a pawnbroker's sign.

Somehow the balls soon mysteriously disappeared.

Never having been to a church garden party and sale, my first experience came as a bit of a shock. For most of the previous week, goods were dumped in the Vicarage and cakes galore handed in which filled all the kitchen shelves. Mr. Proctor, who had been a marine engineer, and now made large working models of railway steam trains, turned up with his son to lay rail tracks round the garden as the engine would be towing a carriage to give children rides. The lawn had been mowed and some parishioners tidied up the flower beds, though they were not too happy about taking on that job when they had plenty to do in their own gardens.

On Saturday I found every room in the house taken over while stalls and goods galore were trailed through the centre passage, from front door to garden door. I had to shut poor Jimp and Goofey in a shed to keep them safe. Dancing girls were to have one bedroom, Boys' Brigade another. Another took the helpers' coats and bags, and men were fixing loudspeakers in our back bedrooms overlooking the lawn. The kitchen and scullery had tea table and cake stall people busy, and the sitting room was fitted up with tea tables, for those wanting tea inside and not on the lawn.

Oh my! Did I get into trouble because I had not noted which cakes were for the cake stall, and which for the teas! This caused a battle throughout the afternoon. 'Tea people' snatched cakes from the stall, and stall holders rushed in to raid the kitchen. There was a battle as to who could have the only tree for their stall to provide a little welcome shade.

By lunch-time very attractive and colourfully decorated stalls had blossomed all over the garden, the train got up steam and donkeys grazed until children came for rides. I persuaded Raymond that we could dash into Tonbridge to get a quick snack meal, since we had no access to food or kitchen. It gave us a brief but welcome breather before Bishop Mann, assistant Bishop, turned up to open the fête.

I was first back into the house while Raymond garaged the car (a Morris 8 given us when our bikes were stolen). As I went towards the kitchen I was asked,

*Hildenborough Garden Party
and Sale in the Vicarage garden.*

"And where do you think you've been? We've looked every where for you."

When told we had been for a quick lunch to Tonbridge, I was ticked off for going away on Sale day.

"Our last Vicar's wife always sat on the stairs and ate a sandwich on sale days."

Raymond heard this and, being pretty tired, told the dear lady off in no uncertain manner, reminding her that this was our home, and it was a kindness on our part to let them take over the whole house for the event. It became known that it was wiser not to tick off the Vicar's wife, whether or not she deserved it.

The Bishop arrived and we escorted him round all the stalls after he had opened the sale with a brief speech in which he expressed admiration for the attractive stalls and for all the work put in by so many.

Having left the Bishop to have tea with some of those attending the Fair, we joined two nuns who had come from the R.C. Convent school directly opposite the church. Evidently there had not previously been such contact with the school, but they had been delighted when Raymond had rung them up the previous week to say we were sad not to be able to attend their garden party, as Raymond would be busy with weddings that afternoon. Our sale gave them a chance to come and meet us, and it was the start of a very friendly relationship with the school, and we enjoyed great Fellowship with the nuns and their Mother Superior. Raymond often had visits from R.C. priests staying on holiday at the Convent.

We were trying to get a church hall built as the dining room was no longer adequate for youth meetings, and great was the joy when we had achieved this. It had been opened by Mrs. Chavasse, and then dedicated by the Bishop. The Convent school was delighted to use it for their speech days, and gave very generous donations for the privilege.

We saw Bishop Mann on to a bus when he left the garden party and sale as he preferred public transport to using a car, and was noted for his knowledge of train and bus timetables. With the departure of Bishop Mann the long, tiring day was coming to an end with the fun of haggling over stall remainders to get the last bargains. Scouts made a wonderful clearance of all litter on the lawn, leaving it showing little effect of all it had suffered during the day.

A Day at Bishopscourt, Rochester

On receiving an invitation from Beatrice Chavasse, to her annual garden party at Bishopscourt for clergy wives in the diocese, I didn't feel too enthusiastic about another garden party. I telephoned Mrs. Russell-White, the Rural Dean's wife, to hear more about this event. I was assured it was a day not to be missed, and she would take me in her car.

The weather was perfect and I enjoyed the drive with other local clergy wives. Mrs. Chavasse was at the door of the Cathedral to welcome us and made us all feel very welcome. I was told how well she remembered Raymond in Oxford, and she had evidently heard our family news as she congratulated me on our forthcoming babe, and wished me well.

After Holy Communion in the Cathedral taken by the Dean, coffee was served in the Palace, giving us a chance to get to know one another, and to discuss parish life and excitements. Conversation flowed so easily, it was hard to realise this was a first meeting for most of us, though we knew the husbands of some who had been our visiting preachers.

I did wish I had been warned this was to be something of an Ascot sort of occasion; everyone wore hats and I had come without a hat. Some said they wished they had been brave enough not to wear a hat, as they had bought one just for this day, and wondered if I had perhaps started others being as brave. Coffee was followed by a talk by a psychiatrist on 'Personality' before we went into the garden to enjoy the picnic lunch provided. Mrs. Chavasse liked to cater as in our busy lives we had to do so much catering.

It was a cheerful and colourful gathering as we strolled round the very large lawns, with a band playing. Bishop Chavasse came over to us saying, "I think this calls for fountains."

I suffered a moment of panic, wondering what we were to do, quickly relieved by seeing him bend down to switch on a nearby garden fountain. Seeing me fussing a friendly dog enjoying crumbs on the lawn, Bishop Chavasse told us he was a visitor, belonging to General Montgomery. Having a great admiration for this famous General, I was delighted to have at least made friends with his dog. The Bishop's twin brother had been an army doctor, rescuing wounded soldiers when under fire, and was killed doing this. He was awarded the VC and bar posthumously. Maybe this was a link between the General and the Bishop.

The delightful day ended with Evensong in the Cathedral, and how I wished Raymond could have been with me to enjoy the wonderful choir accompaniment such as we had once enjoyed in Bradford Cathedral. Tea was served in the Palace before we made for our cars, and we all left hoping to be in the Diocese to enjoy another such gathering. We were made to feel all one great family, made so welcome and so well cared for by the Bishop and his wife. I'm sure not one of us missed having a talk with them both. How very weary they must have felt at the end of the day, yet they were to face another such occasion, as there were too many wives in the diocese to entertain on the same day. I was no longer surprised that Bishop Chavasse ranked as one of the great Bishops.

Sorrow and Joys

The year had a sad ending for Raymond and me, when toxaemia ended my pregnancy in the sixth to seventh month, on Christmas Eve; the babe died in the womb and was removed by caesarian section. I came round from the anaesthetic close to midnight, to find I had been moved from the single darkened room into the maternity ward. As Christmas Day approached the nurses were carrying in babes to their Mums to hear joyful carol singing by nurses processing in with their red cloak linings uppermost. As I woke to the realisation there was no babe for me, I turned away and tried to return to sleep hoping soon to be allowed home.

The Christmas day jollity on the ward was not easy to enter into, and when my surgeon had carved the ward turkey, he came across to my bed with his daughter who was in training as a gynaecologist. He talked of my experience, and his daughter expressed sympathy and said she was sure I'd be luckier next time. Her father quickly added, "Oh no, she must not embark on more pregnancies."

I refused to be dismayed. I had to muster up a cheerful spirit somehow, as Raymond was to come in to see me later. I clearly remembered sitting in Bradford Cathedral, waiting for service to begin. Just in front a young Mum was helping little ones to find places in the prayer and hymn books. As I thought to myself how lovely it must be to have little ones to bring up to know God, this sudden knowledge came to me, "You will be a mother of two children who will grow up to love God."

Once again it seemed most unlikely, but I treasured these strange experiences in my heart. I felt this experience was meant to see me through this challenge. The Lord was my Shepherd indeed. I was relieved to be moved to a single medical ward the next day, as Dr. Rankin was now to take me on. I did not then know that Dr. Rankin's treatment for high blood pressure was to give patients a long rest. I rested there for three winter months. Raymond had to brave ice and snow to reach Tunbridge Wells, but managed to do so every day. As Easter approached I got Raymond to see Dr. Rankin, to ask if I might now be allowed home. He agreed, saying that knowing how busy Vicarages were he was afraid I would not rest if allowed home. The homecoming was not made easier for all the kind sympathy I met with, and there was the empty cot and a pram and all the snow-white nappies to deal with. Pram and cot were quickly sold and nappies sent to a missionary station in Africa, though I hadn't given up hope of the joy of replacing them one day, but Dr. Rankin wanted me to visit him for two years before deciding whether I should risk further pregnancies. Mother told me that she had asked the hospital if my babe had been normal or handicapped. The nurses would not discuss it with me and expected me to forget it had happened. Mother told me it was a daughter, and the nurse told her it was a very beautiful babe, and perfectly normal. I never learnt how her dear little body was disposed of but have since read that they are buried in hospital grounds.

After two long years Dr. Rankin said I must not have further pregnancies. I told Dr. Davison I would like a second opinion, and he sent me to a Harley Street specialist who said I could try again, but to be prepared for the pregnancy to be terminated if trouble arose early on. The second pregnancy ended in a fourth-month miscarriage.

Meeting a parishioner in the village one morning, she stopped to commiserate about the loss of our two babies.

"Does it make you wonder if God is perhaps saying He does not want you to have a family, to enable you to spend more time on the Church family?"

I laughed and said, "No, I am sure God does not work like that."

I did know there were those in the parish who still thought Vicars had wives to be unpaid curates.

In August that year we were invited to holiday with a Vicar's family in Jersey. Edward Richardson had been at college with Raymond and Raymond was Godparent to his youngest daughter. During a delightful week with them, I began to suspect I might again be pregnant. I had a great appetite suddenly and persuaded Raymond to take evening walks with me, so that I could have a fish and chip supper!

On returning home the pregnancy was confirmed and, through taking much rest all went well. How we rejoiced when Elisabeth Anne arrived safely on 18th April, 1956. My consultant took very good care of me and became a good friend. I was in touch with Mr. Grasby until he died in the 1990s. Another very good friend, Mrs. Gladys Fraser, who lived at 'Mountains', a Manor House near us, employed for us a qualified nurse, trained at Great Ormond Street Hospital, to care for Elisabeth for her first few weeks. Elspeth Lunn quickly became one of the family; Elisabeth thrived under her care, and was known to the parish as their special prayer baby.

After Elizabeth's Baptism by Bishop Mann.

Help with parish and family

When I had had my long stay in hospital and returned to church life, I had been intrigued to watch a young man in the front pew during an evening service taking little part but looking angry about it all. I was not too surprised to see him walk straight into the vestry after Raymond. When I was in the church hall having a coffee before the Youth Fellowship meeting I was approached by this young man. He wanted to know if I was satisfied the Vicar was doing a good job. I asked him why he asked this. "I think he's pretty slack. He doesn't do much visiting around the parish. I'm in the new estate and I doubt if he has visited anyone there." I asked how long he had been in Hildenborough, and how often he came to church. He said he was a Methodist, but was now coming to the Anglican church as there was no Methodist church in the village. I told him that not everyone realised how much a Vicar was expected to fit in in a day, and there is a team of lay visitors to cover much of the parish to keep the Vicar informed of who needs a visit, and these people take much of the Vicar's time.

I confessed to him that as Vicar's wife my opinion of him was heavily biased in the Vicar's favour, and went on to explain the difficult months Raymond had had through the winter while I was in Hospital. He told me his name was Brian Newman and he was sorry to have let off steam about the Vicar, and if he could be of any help he would be delighted to do anything he could to extend the influence of the Church in the village. I suggested he could seek election to the P.C.C. if he would like to be confirmed and become an Anglican. He decided to do this and was at once a great help. He undertook to visit round the new estate and, finding some agnostics, invited them into his home to meet the Vicar. At that time an Australian Clergyman, assisting Raymond while in the Parish, went with Raymond for an evening's discussion with the agnostic friends. It was a stimulating and encouraging meeting and some decided to give the church a try, and became regular attenders, some with wives and children. Two or three wives stopped outside church to ask how they could find their way through the prayer book and were amused to find they could soon pick it up by following the 'rubrics' between canticles and prayers etc. They soon mastered that and enjoyed regular attendance. Those were days when not everyone had a car, few had T.V., there were few entertainments and no sport on Sunday, and children were accompanied to church or taken to Sunday School. Raymond was surprised and delighted that twelve church members decided to attend a diocesan conference in Hayward's Heath, and all returned greatly encouraged in Faith by the experience.

The Following Friday, these twelve, who had been thrilled with the conference, all just happened to drop in to the Vicarage that evening without pre-arrangement and were amazed to see each other there. Brian explained that every night of the week each had turned up in one of their homes without pre-arrangement. They thought they were being guided by the Holy Spirit to meet together. Brian suggested we all got together at his home the following evening and to seek guidance with prayer as to how God wanted them to respond to the help they had had at the conference and this Fellowship created amongst them. Brian's idea was that we should be prepared to pray together all night if so led. (Raymond hoped it would not be all night as he had to prepare for the Sunday services.)

We broke up after 10 pm. having enjoyed inspiring Fellowship and frank discussion. There were those who decided to meet at the Vicarage every Sunday morning at 7am to pray for the services and the challenge of the gospel to the congregation. We readily agreed to this, saying the door would be open and the sitting room available, and we would be with them in Spirit. After their prayer session they sat together in church to pray for Raymond's ministry as well as the congregation. Soon great things happened.

One young couple, Ian and Audrey, asked Raymond if he would take Ian through confirmation preparation, as he was not yet a convinced Christian, but Audrey would only marry him if he was secure in his Faith. The sessions with Raymond helped him and Ian was baptised, confirmed and very soon after he and Audrey were married. They took over a horticultural business and their helpers were soon keen Christians helping them with a great work of evangelism in the local village church.

Brian and Jean Ash, who had recently been married in Hildenborough Church and helped with youth work, dropped in to see us at tea-time one evening. Brian came with the news that he had been accepted for training for the Ministry. Though a joy for Brian, Jean was not so happy. Her father and brother-in-law were priests, and Jean was not so keen to 'Join the club'. Jean hoped to give up teaching and start a family. With Brian leaving his good bank job, and going to college, Jean would be obliged to carry on working for several years. Jean felt pressure was being brought to bear on young men to become ordained. To us, it seemed the Holy Spirit was at work in our church. When Raymond got up to return to his study, Jean followed to talk over her worries with him. When she rejoined us, her worries were over. She said as she spoke with Raymond, she suddenly felt happy about this change in their lives.

When, soon after, she found she was in fact pregnant, Brian's father bought them a house to use until they had a church house, because they would have to leave their 'Bank' house, and the Parish felt it an honour to have two of their members training for the Priesthood and decided to help to support Jean financially when she gave up work. During Brian's training years, Jean presented him with a son and a year or so later twin son and daughter. Jean reminded me I had once said to her "God is never in debt to us, He always repays double for any little sacrifice we feel we make for Him!"

When Elisabeth was almost a year old I was assured by my doctor a second pregnancy was unlikely to be a problem, but I was well ticked off by my consultant when he was told that I was four months pregnant, and my Doctor also rebuked. When Dr. Davison came to see if I was worried, he was relieved to find I was overjoyed we had not consulted him earlier as I might not have had my second daughter. I had to take so much rest that it was a busy time for Raymond and my mother.

Erica Rutland, near neighbour and great friend, was always ready to give any help, ironing surplices, helping with "occasions", or taking charge of Elisabeth, either in her home or taking her for walks. Erica told me she had taught Elisabeth to sing 'Daisy, Daisy' when out on walks as her rattly dolls pram always got her singing 'Onward Christian Soldiers', sung all through in perfect pitch, to the astonishment of passers-by, while Erica explained, "She is the Vicar's kid." 'Daisy Daisy' was simply amusing.

I told Erica of Elisabeth who, at a hairdresser's in Weston-super-Mare, was asked if she liked being by the sea, but was unprepared for Elisabeth to sing right through, 'I do like to be beside the Seaside.' The assistant was delighted and asked for the hairdriers to be switched off so that all the customers could enjoy the songs. Elisabeth was very shy when they all clapped.

In March 1958 Sara Gillian arrived safely, providing Elisabeth with a sister, not altogether appreciated by her in the early weeks, but when Mrs. Fraser again so kindly provided a nurse, Sister Speight, to care for Sara in her early weeks, saved Elisabeth from feeling neglected. Sister Speight was happy to help with both children when we had meetings of one sort or another in the Vicarage. It was especially appreciated when Raymond arranged a reunion of local clergy, most being friends of his college days. We entertained the former college Principals, Bishop Chavasse, now our Bishop of Rochester, and his great friend Bishop Taylor, retired Bishop of the Isle of Man. It was an informal reunion of Oxford days. The meeting lasted all day, breakfast, lunch and tea being provided. One of the clergy hearing Elisabeth crying, came and took her into the meeting which cheered her and me, as I was having to neglect her.

Villages in Mourning

Raymond and I felt that the reason why Mr. Grasby's advice to Dr. Davison to warn me against further pregnancies, was quite blotted out in Dr. Davison's memory was because of the very sudden and tragic death of Guy Davison. To us it seemed no time since Guy had joined his father's practice, and they were so happy working together. Not long before Dr. Davison and Guy had attended Raymond together, after an abcessed tooth had caused Raymond to faint when taking Matins one Sunday morning. Stanley Davison had Guy with him to give Raymond an anaesthetic, while a dentist came to remove the offending tooth. (This was on Coronation Day when we had hoped to be with the Davison family watching the Coronation service on their television). The tooth abscess was thought to have been near enough the brain to cause the faint. Raymond was not feeling well when he went into church, but his sudden faint had shocked the congregation – a choirman just managed to catch him as he fell. I shall always remember the choirboys' eyes widening as the Vicar was carried by choirmen through the chancel into the vestry, and was told by a parent later that her boys went home and spent the morning in the garage wrapped in white sheets, acting the Vicar fainting. Others told me there happened to be an ambulance outside the church and someone spread a rumour that the Vicar had fallen from the tower and had been taken to hospital. I noted with amusement that by the time I got to the Vicarage, there was already a basket of fruit, a pheasant and a bottle of brandy to help the Vicar's recovery, sent by Mrs. Fraser. If a member of the congregation fainted they were generally given a glass of water.

The sudden disastrous death of Dr. Guy Davison was a great sorrow to the whole neighbourhood, caused by Guy when out on a shoot, getting the trigger of his gun caught on a fence under which he was scrambling; he was shot through the heart and died instantly. His wife Maisie was a beater also out with him. Devastated as he was, Dr. Davison went on Guy's round of patients in nearby villages the next day, Sunday, so the news had not reached these folk and all greeted Stanley with, "Oh, we were expecting your son," and having to be told the sad news.

Going into church on the day of Guy's funeral, Maisie was making artistic flower arrangements, and said, with amazing composure, "Ours was the perfect marriage in every way, and somehow I had thought it was just too perfect to last." Flowers poured in and were arranged round the church and churchyard. The church overflowed with mourners and there were crowds praying outside. Raymond had gratefully accepted help with the service from local village clergy.

All the local churches raised funds as a memorial to Guy and, when presented to the family, they used it to have cherry trees planted all along the main road in Hildenborough as a living memorial.

Nine long months after Guy's death his son, young Guy, was born to Maisie. While in the Nursing home one can sadly imagine how it must have felt to Maisie, while thrilled to have Guy's son, to see other fathers coming in to see their new offspring. When Maisie's children had grown up, Maisie remarried happily.

Anne, Raymond, Sara, Elizabeth and Jimpey.

Changing Scenes of Vicarage Life
• •

Some of the young Mums in the parish rather envied me having, as they thought, my husband in the home a lot, and working mainly on Sundays, they not being very involved in church activities. While sympathising with those whose husbands were out at work many hours of the day, I did in fact possibly see less of my husband. When he was not out visiting homes or hospitals, he was generally writing letters or talking for societies or schools, or at meetings. Sunday was possibly our easiest day as we had a routine organised for us, though Raymond was taking the 8 am Communion and then taking a service at a farm colony for handicapped men and women. He always had to take an organist with him, and this Mrs. Bampton was a regular church member, noted for the wonderful cakes she could produce for any special occasion. Mrs. Bampton always referred to Raymond as James Mason when talking to me. She was a good friend and made the baptism cakes for Elisabeth and Sara, giving each decorated with a stork carrying a baby which I preserved for use on the cakes of Elisabeth and Sara's babies' baptism cakes, having been told I must do this.

Though some of the men and women at the colony were somewhat mentally retarded Raymond found them to be very spiritually alive and was able to prepare them for Confirmation. When preaching he was warned not to be too humorous as it was very difficult to stop some laughing when once they started. Raymond grew fond of this 'family' and they of him. It could be a bit embarrassing when he met them out, all together, in shops, as they told everyone he was their Vicar, and would all be patting him on the back, and made it difficult to be able to move on. One of the men made a very good dolls' house for the girls and another made a 'stable' for the girls to house their Christmas Nativity set!

Following the Colony service was Matins at Hildenborough Church. Once a month there was a Children's service, which often included a Baptism during the afternoon, when the Sunday School took on duties, perhaps reading a lesson or taking a prayer or taking the collection. This prepared them for regular church attendance. St. John's was quite popular for weddings which mostly took place on Saturdays. This involved taking preparation classes for the couples. Sundays ended with Youth Fellowship meeting after Evensong.

On many a Sunday we were entertaining visiting preachers, and quite a lot of Bishops came to preach. Bradford Cathedral Provost John Tiarks and his wife Gwyneth visited when they could, and used the Vicarage for a brief break sometimes if we had to be away. It was a special joy for me when Bishop Karney, retired Bishop of Southampton, came as representative of the Missions to Seamen. He had once served as their chaplain. I at once recognised him as the Bishop by whom I was confirmed in Bournemouth, when I was sixteen years-old. It had been a special service for me, and I could still remind him of much of his sermon at that service. He became a friend and paid us several visits and was very taken with little Elisabeth. He played with her and carried her around, and said he wished he could place his hand on her head and give her his blessing but was afraid she might think she had been confirmed. When she was leaving church in her pram after service, while talking to people leaving, he hung his Pectoral cross round her neck. She accepted it as a help to her teething, so he removed it before she made any dents in it. (Was his love of Liz a help in her decision many years later to become a C. of E. Priest?)

A Bishop of Lahore, India, who had been at College with Raymond, came to preach one Sunday when Raymond woke up with laryngitis. Though the Bishop was no longer taking services very often, he managed Matins well, apart from having difficulty in remembering the wording of the calling of marriage banns, his version being a little different from the usual. The Bishop was accompanied by his wife and their two young sons who were boarded with an ex-Missionary lady in Hildenborough. I was very relieved when friend Flo turned up unexpectedly from London for the day. She helped me to get the lunch cooked for the seven of us. We offered soup, roast beef and several vegetables, and finished with apple pie and cream, and then cheese and biscuits. The boys tucked in enthusiastically and, when coffee was served complained to Mum, "We are starving, have you got any biscuits?" We had tried to persuade the Bishop to carve the joint, but he wanted us to do it, I was relieved Flo did a good tidy job of carving. Much as we enjoyed meeting this family, as Raymond had been at college with the Bishop, entertaining and doing the catering left us quite relieved that they seemed to have enjoyed their visit though only getting a brief glimpse of Raymond in bed.

The visits of two deeply spiritual persons, Godfrey Mowat, and later, Dorothy Kerin, much used of God in Spiritual Healing, did much to strengthen the faith of many in the parish who attended a Service of Healing led by Godfrey Mowat. We heard many stories from some at the Services, of the great help they experienced from the Faith and the laying on of hands by Godfrey at a special service in Hildenborough Church. Godfrey seemed very closely in touch with God and, though blinded when young, travelled far and wide to be the instrument of healing and renewed Faith for many in a most miraculous way. This deepened the Fellowship in the church and was a blessing to us all.

In August we were able to take a break while church meetings shut down for holidays. Aunt Mabel having offered us her flat in Bournemouth for two weeks, we were very grateful. In August life was at its quietest, and we were lucky that a former Bradford Boys Brigade Officer, now a clergyman, was happy to use our Vicarage for a holiday during our absence, and agreed to help with Sunday services. Albert and Joyce had two very young sons, so preferred to have a Vicarage to themselves rather than to have to holiday with relatives. They had a very demanding parish and needed the break.

We had a very good spell of holiday weather, and all enjoyed the well kept stretches of sand. Sara kept us on our toes, as she was at the crawling stage, and her ambition was to crawl rapidly down to the sea. Liz found the sands more enjoyable. A very restful, relaxing holiday sent us back to Hildenborough feeling revitalised and eager to return to parish activity.

A pile of correspondence awaited our return, and Albert and Joyce had left a letter of thanks. They were quite overwhelmed by the great welcome they received and the invitations into many homes, and some took them on outings. Reading this we were a bit puzzled by the note left in our visitor's book: 'Sorry to leave our second home, for the last time.' Was once enough for our parish, or were they perhaps to move soon to a far away parish?

As soon as we were unpacked and babes tucked up in bed, I went into the kitchen to get us supper, and Raymond took all the mail into the study to sort out. When he rejoined me he said it was an interesting lot, but I was too sleepy to take much note, and was glad to roll into our own bed, leaving a fair bit of sorting out for the next day.

The next morning over breakfast, I asked Raymond what was so interesting in the mail he looked through last night. "I have had an offer of another Simeon trustee parish. This one is in Barrow in Furness, on the north-west coast, in Lancashire. A town that goes in for much shipbuilding as its major industry. The name to me sounded 'in Furnace' and I had a mental vision of the 'black country'.

Raymond had had offers of other parishes while we were in Kent without feeling it was time for a move, but I realised this was different. He clearly felt this was an offer to consider. I was not sure I would welcome a move. Hildenborough had become quite special after eight years; our first home, and where we became four in family, and all our good friends had become very much family.

I thought back to Bradford days – Dark satanic mills, cobbled streets, thick black winter fogs. Working in the hospital I remembered not quite daring to tell the somewhat temperamental orthopaedic surgeon, Ian Lawson Bick, that he had very dirty black smudges on his face after going in and out to different wards in such a grim fog. I laughed when, on returning to my office past a mirror, I saw my face just as grubby. Mr. Dick had refrained from telling me. It was a day when buses were not running, I had succeeded in crossing the road with the help of a torch held low to find the other pavement. I had just set off down the pavement keeping close to the kerb with the aid of the torch, when a broad Yorkshire voice exclaimed excitedly, "Hey up, it's a bus." There was such giggling when I assured the approaching voices, "It's O.K. I'm not a bus!" Such memories made me wonder if we were to leave the Garden of England, for more of this.

I realised Raymond could not come to a decision about St. Paul's Barrow, unless he went to see the church and parish and had met the Church wardens. While Raymond looked through his diary trying to find a free two or three days when he might travel North, I was wondering how I could accompany him. Who could I ask to look after the children and the dogs and cope with callers in our absence?

People in the parish must not suspect we considered a move. I suddenly thought of Phyllis Speight who lived in Sevenoaks, who had been the nurse who looked after Sara for her first few weeks. Phyllis had those days free and readily agreed to come and look after things for us while we had a few days off. Parishioners knew we had plenty of friends in the North so it didn't surprise them to know we were having a brief break up North.

A few days before we set off we had the very sad news from Joyce Clifford, so recently holidaying in Hildenborough Vicarage, to tell us that Albert, her husband, had been killed returning home late at night after a late hospital visit to sit with a dying parishioner. Some drunken youths had run their van into his motor bike. Church members who had much enjoyed Albert and Joyce and their little boys while at the Vicarage, at once responded by sending money with their sympathy. One parishioner sent a generous allowance to help Joyce get back to teaching. Joyce told us that Albert's last sermon was about not fearing death, but to look forward to the next life. This made her wonder if Albert had had a premonition about his death. It was hard for Joyce to understand how God could allow this, leaving two little boys without a Dad, in such a cruel way.

Since Hildenborough parishioners knew about our love of the North and that we had many friends up there it was not a surprise that we should take these few days off. Though I was reluctant to leave the babes, I knew they were in very good hands, and we thoroughly enjoyed the relaxation of the train ride to Lancashire. My father had been born in Lancashire and I had heard him many times wishing to get back to the North. I decided if we moved Dad would have been glad to think of his grandchildren living in Lancashire.

When we reached Grange-over-Sands the country and sea views were most inviting and the very modern Barrow station had no look of the Bradford post-war dark mills. As we left the platform we were met by George Higham, Vicar's warden, and people's warden Horace Hayhurst. Horace had to leave us after a few minutes talk as he was due to take a woodwork evening class. We went with George to his car (with appropriate number plate 'Deo') and he took us to his home. We met his wife Pat, who had a delicious meal all ready for us. We were then taken to see the church, and a choirman member of the church took me round it while Raymond and George had a talk. I asked if the church was a conservative evangelical congregation, (noting the lack of candles on the holy table) and did they have the Communion service taken from the North end of the Holy table? I liked his reply, "I don't think so, but I honestly don't think the congregation would mind if the Vicar took the service on his head if it was taken reverently!

The next morning we were taken on a tour of St. Paul's parish and the daughter parish of St. Aiden's. At St. Aiden's we met the priested curate, who was keeping the services going at both churches with help from the Deacon curate Gordon Lambert, as their Vicar had died of a sudden heart attack. It had been hard work for Marcus, and he seemed ready to leave with the arrival of a new Vicar. Gordon had yet to be priested and was not ready to move. He had a wife, Freda and a baby daughter.

We were given a pleasant tour of the neighbourhood, and shown the shipbuilding area and saw the start of the building of a large liner, the Oriana. All most interesting and we loved the extensive sandy beaches at Walney Island. This was certainly no smoky industrial city. A wonderful open-air feel and wide, tree-lined streets greatly impressed us. The fact that it was very handy for trips to the Lake District, as it was quite easy to spend a spare afternoon in Coniston or Windermere was also a pleasant prospect. Rather more than these added attractions were the very cheerful and friendly people we met everywhere. There was such an infectiously optimistic and joyful attitude to life, and this made us feel we would enjoy working with these church members, and there was plenty of challenge in all that St. Paul's P.C.C. wanted to achieve over the next few years. While Raymond spent an evening with the P.C.C members, I spent the evening with members of the Women's groups. We both found it a happy time.

A very small semi-detached Vicarage did pose us a problem! Mr. Higham and Mr. Hayhurst appreciated our house problem when we explained that Raymond's elderly parents were, with reluctance, leaving their lovely Sussex home to come and live with us. Both in their late eighties they were becoming a worry to supporting neighbours. The Vicarage had a small bedroom at the top of the stairs, and a front double bedroom, the little box room at the back of the house could be made to take two cots, and a double room for us, so there was just sleeping room for us all, and the little single room for the visiting preachers. If family came I supposed we could move the cots into our room. Though this was crowded, the downstairs was as bad. The front sitting room would be needed by Raymond for his office and to accommodate all his book and files, and to allow room for interviews. That left a small breakfast room for family meals, high chair, playpens and toys. The small sitting room would be used for meals when feeding visiting clergy, necessitating the table folded and chairs put aside after meals, to allow visitors to sit round the fire for after-lunch coffee.

After our large Hildenborough Vicarage I did not view this new home with enthusiasm. I told Raymond to tell this to the Patron when replying to the invitation to move to Barrow. The church wardens said they would raise the problem with the P.C.C. It would be a costly exercise to rebuild the old Vicarage, bombed during the war, but they still owned the grounds.

When the church wardens saw us off at the station, we all hoped we would soon meet again. Certainly we felt a strong pull to work with these delightful church members, though St. Paul's church was a Victorian building which had never been completed. As we travelled home we had a lot to consider, and more or less decided that we would leave Hildenborough for Barrow-in-Furness. If there was promise of a new Vicarage we could probably get by with the small semi-detached house for a short while. ,

Arriving back at the Vicarage, we got a great welcome from the girls and the dogs; Sister Speight had been happy with the children and they with her. As soon as it was known we were back a friend rang Raymond, to see if he could visit her as she had some good news for him. He went straight away to find a nice little A40 Austin car which parishioners had bought for us. They were all concerned that our old Morris 8, 'Percy', was not safe for taking the children out; it was so rusty one could sit in the back looking at the road through the rust holes. This presentation was a great embarrassment to Raymond as we were likely to leave the parish. However, he felt he had to tell in confidence that we were possibly about to leave Hildenborough. This was a disappointment to both, as the good lady said she didn't think the donors would want to give the car to one just about to leave. How she could explain this without being able to tell the real reason we couldn't guess, though she said she would keep our secret as it was not then settled.

A few days later John Tiarks let Raymond know that the P.C.C. at St. Paul's, Barrow, would be very happy if Raymond would accept the living, and Raymond said we would be very happy to accept the parish. John Tiarks set the date of Raymond's Induction as 16th September.

Time for a change

Our sadness at having to refuse the generous parish gift of a car, was relieved when Raymond's Father gave Raymond permission to choose a new car for going North, being worried at the state of our Morris 8 for doing long journeys. Raymond's parents still owned a house in Blackheath. He had just recovered it in terrible condition after having been requisitioned during the war. He sold it for a fraction of its former worth but there was enough to pay for a new car for us.

With great excitement we read lots of pamphlets about many different makes of car, and we never regretted our decision to have a Morris 1000 Traveller. It had space for our dogs behind the back seat. That seat easily folded down for transporting chairs from hall to church, or clutter being kept after sales, and so on. It also served as a sleeping area for Elisabeth and Sara while they were small, when we set off very early on long journeys south. Tucked up in sleeping bags they often slept throughout.

The Tonbridge Caffyn's salesman enjoyed our excitement as we each had a trial drive with him when he delivered the car. It was a sad moment when he took away our beloved Percy. Poor Percy was so rusty he had to go for scrap, but we were paid enough to buy new car cushions, as a memorial to Percy.

I really enjoyed a car with four gears after having pushed Percy up hills in Wales, Devon and Scotland on holidays. The children were not thrilled. They didn't like the smell of plastic seat covers after Percy's leather ones. The dogs did however appreciate more room, after being cramped on the floor of old Percy.

The Induction fixed for 16th September didn't give much time for packing up and deciding how much furniture we could take from our mansion to the much smaller house.

Mrs. Grover who had been a great help to me in Hildenborough, enlisted by Mother to help me in the house when I was made to have so much rest, was a great support helping me to pack up.

When Raymond made the announcement of our proposed move to Barrow-in-Furness, some of the congregation were quite dismayed and sad to be losing Raymond, but some took it in their stride and were quite looking forward to a change, hoping to recover the 9 am half-hour service they still missed while others looked forward to a real Vicar's wife, who would give more help with church activity. (A PCC member told me that they were telling the Patron they wanted a married man, but hopefully with a grown up family or perhaps even no family.)

For our part we never found it easy to uproot from a parish, especially one where we had been so happy and where we had met such kindness and affection. We were soon caught up in lots of social calls to say our farewells and with promises on our part that we should find time to come and see them, and on their part that we should be daily in their prayers.

Raymond thought it right to move on because there were always parishioners who had not responded to one Vicar's ministry who might find great help from the next. I recalled a retired clergyman who did not appreciate Raymond's ministry who had taken Evensong the day Raymond had fainted in the morning service. His opening sentence was, "They who wait upon the Lord shall renew their strength *and not faint.*" This caused a few audible giggles.

On the Sunday following the announcement of our impending move, Mary Hicks, widow of the recently deceased Vicar of St. Paul's, Barrow-in Furness, introduced herself as she was leaving church. Mary had been told by the Vicar of the church she now attended in Tunbridge Wells about Raymond having accepted her former parish, so she decided to attend St. John's, Hildenborough to check up on St. Paul's new Vicar. Mary came over to our Vicarage for a chat and we were delighted to hear about St. Paul's and were impressed by the courage she showed as she told us of the sudden death of her husband and having to move within a short space of time. This was the start of a very good long friendship with Mary and her family.

Raymond was about to have a day of entertaining clergy friends for a day, which always meant giving them meals. As Mary knew few clergy in the neighbourhood, and was not yet known to the Bishop, she readily agreed to help me on this occasion. Mary and I had a busy day, and at tea time we mingled with the guests and Raymond introduced Mary to the Bishop, and we had a talk with Beatrice Chavasse who told us their first Parish was St. George's in

Barrow-in-Furness. She was very interested to hear news of Barrow churches from Mary and told me she was still in touch with the widow of their churchwarden of their days at St. George's Church and asked if we would look her up and pass on her greeting to her, which we promised to do, once we had found our way around in Barrow.

Mrs. Chavasse was concerned to hear Mary had a daughter, Alison, aged thirteen years, and a son aged eleven years, and her youngest daughter aged three years. (Little Sarah was playing happily with our little three year-old Elisabeth) and Mary had had a handicapped young son who had died soon after her husband. Mary remained a great friend, and paid us many visits with the family, in Barrow.

On 5th September 1959 it was a strange feeling to think this was our last Sunday of services in Hildenborough, with Raymond as Vicar. There was a large attendance at all services, and we felt we were parting from a large, well loved family after our eight years with them. My mind was full of the memories of moving into our first home, memories of aborted pregnancies and the joys of the births of Elisabeth and Sara. Hildenborough would always remain a special place in our memories and it was sad saying all the goodbyes after the services.

After the farewells outside church following Evensong some of the Youth Fellowship and some older members came back to the Vicarage with us. The Youth Fellowship members said they were coming to help us to 'wreck the joint' as they so nicely put it. In no time, the curtains were coming down, pictures removed and dusted, carpets rolled up and furniture moved to assist the lorry loading. All helped in every way they could to help speed our get away the next day. When all that could be achieved had been done, we settled to enjoy our last cup of tea together before having a final time of prayer. Tired and somewhat deflated, most of us were misty-eyed as we parted.

Tim Baynes, the last to go, said he was coming to Barrow for the Induction, and as he was driving up, he was happy to take care of

Scatty and Goofey and transport them in his car in a rabbit cage. He hoped to race us to the new Vicarage, as we were staying a night in Weston-super-Mare, with my Mother and Sisters. Jimp would travel with us in our new Morris Traveller boot as much personal clothing etc. would be in cases on the roof.

After a fairly short night and after the furniture had been loaded, we said our farewells to the wardens and handed over the Vicarage keys and drove to Weston-super-Mare where Mother had a meal and beds ready for us. We all retired to bed early as Cara was to drive Mother and Jill to St. Paul's Vicarage, setting off very early the next day, to see the furniture unloaded. Raymond gave Jimp an early short walk down Weston Boulevard, while I got the children up and fed, and repacked our cases, and we set off at a more leisurely pace than Cara, Jill and Mother. The Churchwardens were at the Vicarage to greet us, having a cup of tea with the family as all was unloaded, and wonderfully arranged for us. Mother had been busy getting the kitchen clutter unpacked and ready for action.

Elisabeth walked round the new home in wonderment, saying in each room of the furniture, "We had one of those in Hildenborough". A new and puzzling experience for her. I was thankful the babes settled happily in their cots in their new little bedroom, and with Jimp lying between the cots for company, as she had always done, they were soon asleep. We none of us were long in following their example as Mother and my sisters had had a long busy day.

Mrs. Preston, a very kind parishioner, called to tell us she had arranged to put up Raymond's parents and look after them for their first week to allow us time to settle in and get unpacked, and to get to know some of the church members. We did appreciate her very kind help, and her thoughtfulness. A cheering start for us newcomers.

BARROW-IN-FURNESS

St. Paul's Church, Barrow-in-Furness

A New Start

• •

Raymond's Induction in St. Paul's Church took place on 15th September, 1959. Sadly Cara and Jill couldn't stay for the Induction as they had to get back to work, and Mother went with them. We had the joy of entertaining John and Gwyneth Tiarks to a meal before the evening service; John Tiarks, while Provost of Bradford Cathedral, was the Simeon Trust representative as patrons of St. Paul's, as they were of St. John's, Hildenborough.

With a very full church, and heartfelt singing led by a choir of eight men and sixteen choirboys, professionally trained by Margaret Taylor, who had been organist and choir mistress for a great many years, the service was impressive, inspiring and joyful. The Bishop of Penrith, suffragen Bishop of Carlisle, the Rt. Revd. Cyril Bulley, led the service and preached. He spoke very warmly of the great ministry of the late Edmund Hay Hicks, who died so young of a heart attack. He welcomed Raymond to the diocese and spoke of the firm foundations on which Raymond could now build. After the service we walked round to the old church school (being used as the church hall) to receive the official welcome from the parish. During the Induction service with the accompaniment of the music of a lovely anthem, my thoughts were in Hildenborough, thinking of that last Induction, and of the loss of babies, and the joyful gift of Elisabeth and Sara, of our youth Fellowship ups and downs, the founding of the Boys' Brigade, and our wonderful, Christian friends from whom we gained so much. I guessed their minds and prayers were with us as much as ours were with them

John Tiarks and Gwyneth, had to leave the reception early, but not before John spoke kindly of Raymond. The meeting went on fairly long as there were so many people to meet, and we were delighted to find how friendly and welcoming they all were, and I felt we should be happy in this parish, as Mary Hicks and her family had been.

On our first Sunday there was a full church, and the congregation was not treated to a sermon by the new Vicar, as he had to 'Read himself in', i.e. had to read the 39 articles of religion (to be found at the end of the *Book of Common Prayer*). This took some time so Raymond was kind in reading only half in the morning and the rest at Evensong. We were in a bit late to lunch having had so many greetings from our new parishioners, and many were saying they hoped to entertain us to a meal very soon. We enjoyed a chat in the Vicarage with the wardens and some of the PCC members over a coffee after service.

Raymond was then on duty and a busy week lay ahead. Each day started at 7am with morning prayer with the curate Gordon Lambert. After a hasty breakfast Raymond would go through the considerable mail before setting off on a round of visits in homes and hospitals. There were some mornings when he took the assembly service in St. Paul's Junior School. On Saints' Days the school attended a short morning service, and then were allowed a day off. For my part I was not really prepared for the complete change in my life. I saw very little of Raymond, and was still unpacking this and that in spare moments, and little Elisabeth was very unsettled by the move and nervous of the strange people constantly coming to the Vicarage.

When walking down the road to the local shops one morning, with Sara in her pushchair, and Elisabeth walking with me, we met a lady, who introduced herself as Mary and her little girl as Bridget. Elisabeth and Bridget were the same age, and Mrs. Martin asked if Elisabeth could come to her house a little way up beyond the Vicarage, on Hawcoat Lane. Mary's older daughter Jane was at secondary school, so Bridget would love a pal her own age. They quickly became friends and they were often in each other's home. This was a help to Elisabeth and she was soon settled in the new parish.

Granny and Grandad Fountain did not settle so easily. They had a lovely home in Sussex, having bought a plot of land near downlands and had a house built to their own design. Over the years they had made a lovely garden, and the trees they had planted were well grown. They had made a pond where herons came hunting for fish. There were plenty of nightingales in the area. (A small wood at the bottom of the garden was where Raymond had proposed to me as we were returning to the house after a downland walk.) I could understand their misery at being unable to cope any more on their own. To adapt to the industrial North, and to a home which was more like an office with people coming in and out at all times, the phone or doorbell a constant interruption and young children cluttering the small breakfast room, they were soon pining for their peaceful Sussex home. In their eighties it was very difficult to adapt happily. I came in for a fair amount of criticism as did the children. It was not easy for any of us, but we tried as best we could.

In retrospect, though we thought it a kindness for the parents to be living with their son when needing help in old age, we later wondered if they would not have been happier in a residential home in Sussex, where they could have kept in touch with many friends and their other son when he was on leave from the Army. It would have been different if Raymond had not had to be out early and late, and unable to spend much time with them. Soon parishioners used to come to visit Mr. and Mrs. Fountain senior, and this was appreciated. Our very kind Doctor Allan, also visited frequently just to see how they were.

The children came to church with me to Matins, and Granny and Grandad were able to come while well enough. The children and I only stayed for the first processional hymn as Sara standing on the pew would shout, "Dad, Dad, Dad," as soon as Raymond started the service. I found it a sacrifice to have to miss Matins, but I wanted the children to know Sunday was a special day of meeting with God, and to get into the church attendance habit, but I did not want them forced to a service which would just see them getting bored and not understanding it, but wanted them to enjoy the outing, and to grow gradually into gaining more from worship.

The congregation liked to see them and appreciated not having them playing up with boredom. By the time they started school they had learnt how to find their way through the *Book of Common Prayer* and were kept happy finding places and trying to sing psalms and hymns.

Getting Down to Work

● ●

Though I was not a member of the Parochial Church Council, I was invited to our first meeting. We met in the old school and there was a full attendance. I was told they would like to co-opt me as a member of the P.C.C. and I was glad to accept membership. I thought back to our first P.C.C. in Hildenborough where the first discussion was how to raise enough money to pay the Vicar. I was glad I did not have the embarrassment of that this time. It seemed there was plenty of enthusiasm in St. Paul's for raising money and we heard of expensive projects. This old school building was to have alterations to make it a fine church hall, by having large rooms to replace the classrooms. The new school was now in full use so work could begin on the hall. The new school was to have an official opening on 30th September, by Viscount Knollys. In the assembly hall a plain oak cross was to be erected as a memorial to the Reverend Edmund Hay Hicks, who had seen to the carrying through of the building of this beautiful and bigger new school, as St. Paul's School always had waiting lists of pupils anxious to be accepted.

On the Sunday, the Bishop of Carlisle, the Rt. Rev'd. Thomas Bloomer, would dedicate the completed school and this tribute to Mr. Hicks who had been present at the dedication of the first part of the school and his widow, Mary, was to attend this occasion on 30th September. We said we would be happy to have her to stay in her former home, as she was already a friend, having come to live near us in Kent. It was further hoped it might be possible to raise money to complete the church building, which had already waited over a hundred years to extend the nave.

The need for a new Vicarage was mentioned and, the fact that the site of the former Vicarage was sometimes sought by local builders keen to buy it from the church, made it seem wise not to delay the rebuilding too long. The old Vicarage had suffered from bombing raids and had been reduced to rubble, but the Vicar at that time was a bachelor who had bought Hawcoat Lane house for his use and then sold it as a Vicarage to the church. This had delayed the rebuilding.

St. Aiden's Church was a dual purpose hall, and the growing congregation made it desirable to build a church, as there was now need for a church and a hall. St. Aiden's was likely to lose daughter church status, in this event, and become an independent church, but would look to St. Paul's for help with the cost of a new church.

Raymond and I were impressed by the positive attitude of the PCC facing all these expensive building needs. The church had a high roof so would be a very expensive project on its own. The council knew they were facing to raise many thousands, but said they managed to dig deeply in their pockets to achieve a fine school and, if they dug a bit deeper, all could be achieved in time. A Finance Committee was appointed to discuss with the Vicar ways of raising money, and they would report back to the next PCC. I was cheered that mention had been made of the need for a new Vicarage, but Raymond could not see that being achieved in any hurry.

The Finance Committee lost no time in getting down to discussing ways to increase giving in the church. They approved Raymond's suggestion that one way would be to amend the Free Will offering, by having envelopes labelled Partner's Scheme, and to suggest to all the congregation, even children, that they should each have weekly envelopes and to give each week according to how God had prospered them. A rise in pay, a windfall, a birthday bonus, or such, or perhaps the opposite, i.e. a week of extra heavy expense, when they could give less. Children who wished might like to give a small amount, even a penny from their pocket money, to feel they were helping to build up the church. In this way no one need feel afraid of having to promise an offering too hard to keep up. With some Free Will offerings some were perhaps encouraged to give on the careful side in case they could not keep it up. No one need fear their giving might be thought too meagre, as their giving would be quite secret, unless people were covenanting and had to declare to the accountant what was to be given. For others the number on the envelope would be recorded in the accounts and this would be known to the accountant, but the names of donors would be known only to the Vicar who would not know the amounts. He would have names and the accountant the numbers and never the twain should meet. Almost all members of the congregation were keen to take part in this effort, and the result were most encouraging.

There were to be the usual sales of work, fairs and tea parties in one another's homes and so on.

Domestic affairs

Once more I was a disappointment to most of the ladies in the parish who had hoped I would take a lead in church organisations, though all were running well with excellent leaders. For a start I was often able to be at meetings, because Granny and Grandad did not mind keeping an eye on the babes for an hour or so, and quite often Mary Martin invited the children to her house to let me attend, as Bridget and Jane were happy to amuse them most of the time. I was thought to be too fussy about not leaving the children too long, but I had had a mother in the home when I was small and felt this was important at least until the children were at secondary school. Besides, I had lost two babes, making these extra special.

Having two babes and two elderly failing parents, all needing help with meals, and the parents needing breakfast in bed, while Sara was still in a high chair, and little Liz not the tidiest eater at three years-old. The tidying up in a cramped house took time, and there were special meals to prepare, and often coffee or tea to produce at the drop of a hat when other clergy came looking for Raymond, or sometimes the Rural Dean, or one of the Bishops looking in on passing. One has to experience Vicarage life to fully appreciate how full life can be. I quite often was addressing envelopes for distributing round the parish, or even delivering some while out with the children.

Jimp needed her walk as soon as the Grandparents were up and Goofey, having had a good breakfast, always shot over the bottom fence to the neighbour's garden. Seeing them in the garden one day

I said I hoped my cat was not digging up their garden, as I saw him scale the fence every morning. "Oh no, he behaves perfectly and he loves his breakfast of scrambled egg each morning; we enjoy his daily visit." I was delighted to hear he even had a bed in their shed in case we were out when he wanted to get in. From then on when we went away on holiday the Miss Browns were always willing to look after Goofey for us. Much kinder than going into a cattery.

Though Jimpey was apparently full of energy and loved a children's play park and would jump on the hand-pushed roundabout they enjoyed, as she chased around with the children, she was not eating well. She would sit and give me long intensive looks as if telling me something. I had a horrible feeling it was time to say goodbye, though she was only eight. I took her to the vet who said she had an internal obstruction which would require an operation. He said we might leave her and he took her into the electrically warmed recovery kennel where she would wake up. Jimp made no move to leave with us but settled down in the straw bed and watched us go. I was then sure she was saying goodbye, but tried not to believe it. The next day I was in bed with a dose of real 'flu when the vet rang to tell me Jimp had cancer and would have died in a day or two, so he had put her to sleep while still under the anaesthetic. I was grateful to Dr. Allan: he was so determined I should have a couple of days rest to recover from real flu he kept me more or less asleep for about three days. I was just conscious of Raymond rushing about in a real tizzy, but I could not come round to get to work. I told Dr. Allan that Raymond had had a very difficult few days of coping with children and parents and trying to see his curate etc. and Dr. Allan simply said, "You had to rest and that was the only way I could make you stay in bed." The pain of losing Jimp was rather worse than the 'flu. Having got over the worst so easily, the children kept asking when they could fetch Jimp from the vet. I found an advert for Border Collie pups for sale on the Scottish borders. I wrote for two, as they had a long train journey to endure. The large bitch pup had a wide white collar, the smaller very black pup had prick ears and was very pretty also. Elisabeth claimed the

The family at St. Paul's Vicarage.

Elizabeth and Sara on Lake Windermere standing on 14 inches of ice.

bigger pup and Sara the small black one, and we called Sara's pup Dusk, and Elisabeth's Dawn. Walking with the pups seeing them undergo training, taught the girls how to train dogs. When I once rescued four sheepdog pups under threat of being killed, as they had not found homes, Elisabeth and Sara were up early before school each day and trained them beautifully on field walks.

But that was some years ahead when they were at St. Paul's Junior School. While they were at the infant school the dogs always came with me to see the girls home. At this time I made a couple of very good friends who were meeting their sons. Pauline Spencer had three boys and Gladys Haley had one son, Richard, who quickly became Sara's great friend. Elisabeth played a lot with the Spencer boys who lived very near us. Peter was the oldest; Nicholas was about Elisabeth's age; Anthony the youngest was often referred to as Ant by the other children but became Tony as he got older. Having these friends meant they were usually in one garden or the other, and allowed more quiet for the grandparents.

Sara (second from right) with her great friend, Richard Haley, at the Infant School, Barrow-in-Furness.

When the dogs were a year old they got jealous and quarrelsome and I decided one must go. I was delighted that Pauline offered to buy Dawn, as the boys loved playing with her, and the boys wished they could have a dog. On the day I was to take Dawn round to them, she escaped as a tradesman had left the door open. I couldn't find her so rang Pauline to tell her. She was about to ring me to tell me Dawn had turned up in her garden, and was playing with the boys. Sheepdogs are amazingly intelligent. The girls helped me to carry round her bed, toys and food bowl and were not unhappy about losing Dawn to the boys as they visited often with Dawn.

I was unhappy that Raymond and I were having to live separate lives for the most part as he was out so much and I was tied to the home most of my time. When Raymond did come in, his parents expected his attention as well as the girls. Matters improved when we engaged a home help two mornings a week. I could then have an hour or two with Raymond while visiting or shopping. I sometimes escaped for a day to attend a Diocesan Conference with him in Carlisle. This involved lovely drives through the Lake District which was a treat for us both. We had constant visitors, and it was a joy when Mother and my sisters could spare a week with us.

Raymond and Gordon were glad when the PCC agreed to the replacing of Marcus Nicklin, curate of St. Paul's Church, since Gordon was occupied with St. Aiden's. Several ordinands came to see St. Paul's, including one from Wycliffe Hall, whom Raymond hoped would join him. At the same time the Bishop was wanting Raymond to take a Carlisle Diocese ordinand whose Father was a Vicar in the Diocese. This Ordinand, John Hancock, was at Durham University, and not keen on working in the same diocese as his Father. He cancelled two proposed visits before deciding eventually to come and meet Raymond, though by this time neither was too interested in meeting the other.

Raymond was busy in the study when I heard the front door bell but, seeing through the glazed door a tall and broad figure dressed all in black, I remembered Mary Hicks warning me about a large tramp who could be very aggressive if refused food or money. I decided to let Raymond answer. It was in fact John Hancock. John was 6'7" tall and was wearing a black rainproof outfit because he had travelled on a motor bike from Durham. From their moment of meeting, Raymond and John got on famously and we never had a more willing and able curate. John soon became one of the family and was often in and out of the Vicarage and quite often joined us for meals. This was a great partnership and John soon had a very large Youth Fellowship. John took a crowd of youngsters each year to a Christian conference in the snow-clad heights in St. John's-in - the-Vale, during the Christmas holidays, where they gained a deepening Faith and strengthened Fellowship. Raymond's one worry about John was that he overworked. He was always ready to do anything to help anyone.

Exciting days

The joint ministry of Raymond and John saw an increase in church membership and the church extension fund was growing encouragingly. Many churches were experiencing new life at the time, and Raymond's preaching was greatly appreciated. Raymond's Uncle and Godfather, Canon Warner, was well known as a great evangelical preacher throughout the country, and was well known for his preaching at Keswick annual convention. Raymond had been much influenced and helped by him as a boy, and as a member of Crusaders got in the habit of much Bible study from an early age. He decided at the age of twelve that he wanted to be a priest. At Wycliffe Hall he had outstanding Christian teachers, and enjoyed great Christian Fellowship with other keen students. Rarely did he miss his daily Bible study, so in his middle years he had a wonderful Bible knowledge, and this understanding of the Faith made his preaching greatly appreciated in all his churches. St. Paul's other great asset at the time was the wonderful church music we enjoyed, thanks to Margaret Taylor, the very professional and talented organist and choirmistress. John's great work with the young people and his popularity all combined to the making of a truly Christian family. Both Raymond and John had good voices for reading and singing the service. Not surprisingly, the church was soon overflowing with congregation and the church extension became more urgent.

In 1963 St. Aiden's became independent of St. Paul's Church with Gordon Lambert as Vicar and its own PCC. About this time when we were having a meal with the Highams, I asked George about the promise of the parish that we were to have a new Vicarage. He did not remember any such promise, but referred to his book of minutes and found it was decided we should have a new Vicarage if we accepted the living. Raymond did not think we should have raised this matter with so much expenditure needed in the parish, but life in the cramped semi-detached Vicarage did not affect Raymond so much as it did me and the children. Granny and grandad Fountain had had to move to a nursing home, as Grandad was found to have cancer and needed nursing help. Sadly he died in the home and Grannie returned home to us in 1961. Granny needed help now. I had the children at school and coming home for lunches, and I found life demanding and tiring.

Mr. Higham was full of apologies for having completely forgotten the promise of a new Vicarage and felt this must be dealt with without further delay. It was very exciting walking along Abbey Road to watch progress on the building. The Diocese made a grant towards the cost, and the sale of Hawcoat Road house raised £3,900, and the new Vicarage cost £8,633. We were to move in in May 1964. The furniture was moved in, but we had a holiday booked to go to a conference on Spiritual Healing held at Lee Abbey in Devon, so we left the bulk of unpacking until we returned. At that time I had a wonderful home help in Mrs. Muriel Westwood. She was a trained Nanny, and had had the care of a Bishop's children before her marriage, but took up domestic work when there was no jobs for Nannies in Barrow. She readily agreed to take the children to Brighton to my Mother, while we were away, and we'd collect them there on our way home.

Having had a very enjoyable and relaxing holiday with family and friends in Guernsey the previous year, the idea of what one might think of as a busman's holiday, spending two weeks with clergy and wives at a religious conference this year was very acceptable. It was a complete change of scene and the routine was very stimulating and beneficial.

The conference speaker, Agnes Sandford, an American greatly used in spiritual healing gave wonderful lectures on this subject. At times her lectures demanded much thought and contemplation, but her sense of humour would break in at tense moments, so that though a bit heavy going at times, the lectures were interspersed with much laughter. Her talk of how she was introduced to healing by prayer, through a young clergyman's prayers for her son, when dangerously ill, resulted in miraculous healing was very inspiring. Quite a number of clergy returned to their parishes inspired to go more thoroughly into the subject, and to start prayer groups for such healing.

There were talks after breakfast by some of the community members of Lee Abbey, and members were ever ready to help with any advice on problems discussed with them. There was much talk about parish difficulties, and a great sense of Fellowship grew up as the days passed. In the afternoon most of us joined walks led by some of the members of the community, or went bathing from Lee Abbey's private beach. Cream teas were sampled by most of us on the walks, and the Devon coast was very lovely to explore.

The two weeks passed all too quickly, though Raymond and I were very much looking forward by then to return to Bournemouth to collect Elisabeth and Sara, to allow 'Wessie' to get home. We followed the day after by car, and as we approached Barrow were thinking we were going to be busy settling into our new home which was very unprepared when we left. A delightful surprise welcome awaited us from the Bible study and prayer group members. On arrival at the new home, despite the tiredness of the long journey, the girls were soon racing round the rooms and in the garden. Raymond and I were astounded to find the house occupied. These good friends had a light meal ready for us and had been hard at work washing labels off the new radiators, washbasins and off the sinks and the new loos. A lovely picture of colourful flowers was already hanging in the hall, with good wishes from Mr. and Mrs. Agar. It was a copy of a picture Raymond had admired in their home. There was a presentation vase with a lovely colourful bouquet just underneath. Chairs were set out in the sitting room as these folk wanted to start our time in the new home with a brief time of prayer of blessing on the new Vicarage. They said they hoped we didn't mind them getting a key and invading, and we hastened to assure them it was a lovely welcome back. We told them we felt they were our family and we hoped they would always feel free to drop in to see us at any time. They had helped to provide this lovely new Vicarage, and I would like them to feel they could come and take roses from the large bed of lovely roses that had been planted under the sitting room window on the front drive.

We were amused when one of the local clergy told us, the other clergy in the town referred to St. Paul's parish as 'Paradise.' Quite an apt description we thought. Much of the garden was newly laid out, but a nice jungle for the children under tall elms was appreciated.

The Vicarage was much as I had planned when consulted by the Diocesan Architect. I had asked for a roomy kitchen to allow for ladies coming in to prepare refreshments for parish parties, and I was also given a utility room with a covered porch outside the back door, having a door to a coal store and a door to the garage, under cover. I had shown the architect the many bookcases Raymond would want to accommodate in his study, so room was allowed for these. I asked for a sizeable dining room as we gave meals to a fair number most weeks, and at Christmas would expect anything up to 16 or 18 round the table, as lonely oldies were delighted to come to lunch to celebrate Christmas in company. In addition to all this I was given five bedrooms as a centre bedroom had a light partition, to give the girls each their own bedroom, but if only four rooms were required in future, the partition was movable. I was delighted that a large airing room with shelves each side was provided for storing bed linen. I used one side as room for the children's many toys, to keep the house tidy. When I had as many as three visitors I had room for the girls beds in our room, which left three bedrooms free. Raymond's mother had a room at the top of the stairs next to the bathroom. It was a wonderful home and Wessie and I decided we must get some new furniture. The Bishop was coming to take a blessing of the new Vicarage, and asked me if I would invite all the local clergy to visit, as well as family and members of the church.

Completion of new Vicarage, St. Paul's.

I had never been to sale rooms so Wessie said she would take me and see that I got some tidy bargains. I was thrilled with all that was on sale, and we decided to try for a three-piece suite in new condition. Arriving early for the sale we got front seats, but when the sale commenced I was a bit dismayed that my chair, a nice high-backed Victorian armchair was needed as the first lot to be sold. I didn't fancy having to stand for the sale, so bid for the chair and got it for 15/-. (Raymond was not too thrilled with it until he sold it some years later for £75.) I was pleased with my purchase and, turning to talk to Wessie, found I had had a parrot cage knocked down to me, thinking I was bidding. I was grateful to the auctioneer for re-selling it. We got the three-piece suite for £30 and left after I had secured a nice mahogany Sheraton dressing table for 1/- because the mirror was missing though the supporting struts were there. These could be unscrewed to leave a pretty chest.

We left early before tempted with any more bargains, though before we left Barrow Raymond had added a lovely large mahogany bureau in perfect condition for £27. Similar ones we saw selling very expensively in second-hand shops in Keswick at the time.

About thirty turned up for the Blessing of the Vicarage by Bishop Bloomer, and I was glad Mother and my sisters came to join the party, and Wessie baked some lovely cakes. Though Granny was not often keen on these parish events she decided to join in this occasion and to meet the Bishop.

Granny Fountain in her 90's was deafer than she knew, so her little asides were spoken rather too loudly, causing embarrassment to some who heard. "Who is the lady over there with a hat like a lampshade?"

Quiet reply: "Mrs. Blunt, the Bishop's wife.

"Is the lady across the room Chinese or is she wearing a lot of make up?"

"She is the lady who has bought our Hawcoat Lane Vicarage. No she is not very made up and she is English."

My sisters took over and chatted to Granny and kept her supplied with cakes, etc. The clergy were all envious of the new Vicarage as most were in large Victorian houses and were impressed that this new Vicarage was roomy, yet far easier to look after. Some clergy in new Vicarages were unhappy that they were too cramped for the job. We had a lovely back garden screened from the main road, but the front had a large lawn area and tall elms along the main road which reduced the traffic noise. We had noisy rooks, but I enjoyed watching their early nesting and care of their young. If a young rook fell from the nest all the rooks were in a great flap and their noise told me they wanted help. Getting the youngster on to a branch was usually enough for them to encourage it to climb higher.

When new young clergy arrived in the town we generally had them in for a meal, and several of the curates took to coming to see Raymond to consult him as to future moves. I suppose Raymond was about the oldest of the local clergy in his early fifties and had been in the Ministry for about twenty years, and he was pleased to be consulted. One newcomer, a young Vicar, dropped in for coffee one evening, and Granny was still up. As they sat down she said very audibly, "When are these people going?" She wanted help upstairs.

The new Vicarage was far easier for entertaining and Granny seemed happier too in less cramped accommodation. We had added two Jack Russell pups to the family, Tops and Towser and Dusk would round them up for me if they raced too far ahead of us in fields. The children greatly enjoyed them, but Granny didn't take to them and never wanted them in the room with her as they were too lively.

There was a lot of taking and meeting of the girls at music lessons, or Brownies, or Ballet classes, so the dogs took exercise with me and were much fussed by friends. Violin lessons for both girls were at school, but Elisabeth started piano and organ lessons with Miss Taylor, and Sara also went to her for piano lessons.

As Granny grew more frail she could not be left alone for long and I was grateful to Mrs. Preston and Mrs. Waring who would often come in to spend time with Granny when I had to be out. I had been accidentally roped in to a local art class run by a professional portrait painter. I had asked about lessons for Victor Harper's wife and I was enrolled with her. This worried me as I'd been told at school to give up art as I was hopeless at it. I was assured it was a lot of fun. When I went to the first class, our tall imposing tutor, Norma Ingram bore down on me asking, "And what do you know about oil painting?

Quite nervously I said, "Absolutely nothing."

"Thank God for that," said Norma. "I shall be able to teach you. I can't teach those who keep telling me, 'But I always do it this way.'

I can't teach those who think they already know it all."

From that moment Norma and I were friends. I loved the painting classes and it filled time at home practising.

Time for a Change of Curate

We were very fortunate that John Hancock had decided to stay at St. Paul's for his four years of curacy so, sadly, John was to move on in 1965. We were delighted he was only moving to Coniston as Vicar. John had married Margaret Hayhurst, daughter of Horace and Hilda. When in Coniston they had two sons and two daughters, and granny and grandad were able to spend much time with the grandchildren being only about half-an-hour away. Happy though we were for John and Margaret the whole parish and the Youth Fellowship, now the membership of over a hundred, were very sad to lose John. His leadership had been wonderful.

I was in to take a phone call from a prospective curate and I invited him to come to lunch with his wife, Jo. He did not seem a bit enthusiastic about coming to Barrow and assured me he was probably older than the Vicar and was not yet ordained Deacon. I told him he was welcome to come and see the parish, so he agreed to come to lunch to meet Raymond.

Raymond had rather hoped for a young man to tackle the large Youth Fellowship, but they decided on meeting that they could work together happily. Victor Harper was in fact a year older than Raymond and they discovered they had both attended the same church in Blackheath when they were boys. They had not met as Victor was a choirboy and Raymond being at boarding school and only at home in holidays. Victor did remember Raymond's father as the church warden who had dragged him out of a tree when Victor was in choir robes trying to reach conkers!

Shortly before John left us he came in to tell us with some amusement that, just loading up their removal van as they were leaving Barrow, he had been offered a pianola by a parishioner to take to Coniston. He had refused it. We told him we'd love it, as the children hadn't a piano and were taking lessons. In next to no time the pianola arrived with lots of rolls to play. The children were delighted, and loved to play the rolls when I had someone in the kitchen, to hear them exclaim at how talented my girls were at the piano. The visitors enjoyed the joke when taken to see the girls working hard with their feet. Miss Taylor came to test the piano to see if it was good enough for the children to practise on and was pleased to find the keys were reasonably stiff to play, and the tone was good. It stood them in good stead for some years.

The children always took an interest in the tramps who came asking for food, and when a big brawny Scot came one morning, the children were fascinated with him and as I was getting him some food and drink, they sat on the front doorstep with him and chatted away to him. They were throwing a ball for Dusk and telling him Dusk would never attack anyone. I kept a wary eye on them through the kitchen window, and they stayed with him while he ate the sandwiches, and then fetched photo albums and stamp albums to show him. He told them he had been very naughty when young but they must always be very good, and never upset their parents by doing things they knew were wrong. He gave them an Alchoholics Anonymous badge and a Methodist church badge and asked them to pray for him.

When about to leave he asked if he could speak to me, and he told me it was the first time he had been able to chat to children since he lost touch with his own two little boys. He had been sent to gaol in his teens for a long sentence, accused of robbery with violence. At nineteen he had married and then got in with a bad lot of lads. He never saw his wife or children again, and if he spoke to any child in passing they were hastily dragged out of his path. It had been a tremendous joy to have the children so eager to chat with him. He was not able now to trace his family and the police still harassed him at the slightest opportunity. He was making his way to London to see if he could get any sort of a job. I suggested he made for St. Martin in the Fields and asked the people who helped folk with no home or work to offer him shelter in the crypt. He seemed interested in this idea. He looked such a decent man and sounded as if he had come from a good family; I felt sad for his wasted life. The girls mentioned him in their night time prayers for some weeks and treasured the badges he gave them – probably all he had to part with.

Many tramps were regulars who would turn up each year and had interesting tales to tell, and seemed to enjoy the freedom of their way of life, but the Scot was a different sort of character, and I hoped he got help to return to a better life.

Ever Pressing On

Bishop Bloomer, Bishop of Carlisle, decided that Victor should be ordained Deacon in St. Paul's Church in December, 1965. Margaret Taylor rose to this challenge as ever with a very well trained choir who had had practice in singing the Litany, as well as wonderful hymns and anthems. Bishop Bulley had often been to St. Paul's, but it came as a surprise to Bishop Bloomer just how professional a choir we had at St. Paul's. In the vestry before the service he was telling the choir that the litany would be sung, and not to worry, he would sing a phrase and they then just copied what he had sung. None of the boys said they could sing the litany so, during the service when they sang it so beautifully, and as well as a cathedral choir, it gave the service a great lift, and they excelled in the anthems and hymns. The music moved Victor to tears in so emotional a service as his ordination. The atmosphere in church was so inspired, it was a very memorable occasion for us all. In the vestry after service Bishop Bloomer told Raymond his choir was better than Carlisle was at that time, and it was a very moving service. He also asked that this comment must not reach Carlisle Cathedral choir.

Victor was worried about having to cope with a very big Youth Fellowship, but in fact numbers were reduced as it was time for many to go to college or into full time work, and when some of the older group left this very often meant other members lost interest and left. Victor soon got on to the wavelength of the reduced number of YF and they progressed well together. Victor's sense of humour made him many friends, some thinking he reminded them of the TV presenter Hughie Green.

Victor arrived at an exciting time in the history of St. Paul's as work was at last to start on the lengthening of the church nave. The completion fund had reached £10,000 with help from a diocesan interest-free loan of £3,000. The contract was signed and in June the building work was started, and by Christmas most of the west wall was completely demolished. A temporary entrance was made in the west wall of the south transept. Though in January a curtain of strong plastic acted as the west wall, this was screen enough against weather to enable use of the church for services to continue. The many prayers for a mild winter were heard, and the noise of the plastic waving a bit in the wind did not prove a problem.

At Christmas the usual extra services, with a 7am and an 8am Holy Communion, followed by the service and then a packed Matins kept us both occupied, and for me there was the task of seeing that enough food was cooked for a Christmas lunch for about fourteen of us, as we now had room to entertain those who liked to come, rather than spending Christmas day alone. Having got the Christmas Pudding on, and the Turkey in the oven, very early, when I switched on the grill to give Raymond breakfast toast, I fused the electric cooker.

I was not keen to get an electrician out of bed early on Christmas day, but in desperation I rang Mr. Forrest, who was father of Sara's boy school friend Peter Forrest. He willingly came round at once and got my cooking going, to my great relief. Making sauces and preparing vegetables kept me busy, but I fitted in Matins before Raymond then went off in the car to collect those coming to lunch, after he had taken a Communion Service following matins. Victor and Jo kept the party lively after lunch, and all watched the children unpacking presents, after they had given to the guests token gifts off from Christmas tree. We handed round musical crackers containing whistles which each contained one note of the scale. Victor conducted by reading the music and pointing his baton to the owner of the note required.

While Raymond and I were doing a clear up in the kitchen and treating the dogs and Goofey to their share of the turkey, we could hear much laughter coming from the whistle concert in the sitting room. The children, having some new board games, filled in time until the Christmas cake and mince pies were brought in. The children were very reluctant to be despatched to bed early, after their early start, but were quickly asleep once settled. Our guests were happy to continue playing board games well into the evening, and it was about 11 pm before Raymond and Victor had seen them safely home, and Jo gave me a hand with the final tidy up. Christmas in Barrow was always shared with guests and provide very happy memories.

1967 Dedication of Church Nave Extension

It was a bit of a heartbreak to have to see Elisabeth off to St. Anne's Boarding School, Windermere, as she had left St. Paul's in the summer. Sara would have missed her more had it not been for friend Richard Haley. They were nearly always together in one home or the other and in the same class at school, so the two years before she could join Elisabeth at St. Anne's School passed happily on the whole.

The other great event in September was the Dedication of the new church extension building. Many were the joys for us in Barrow, but one day that stands out in the memory of all of those at the dedication ceremony that evening, is a memory that will not fade with time.

All four hundred of the new seats were full and the Mayor and Mayoress and their deputies were there to enjoy this long awaited occasion. Raymond had worked out an impressive service in which the Bishop played the main part, hammering the new door with his pastoral staff to be let in to dedicate the new work. The builder was

St. Paul's Church, Newbarns and Hawcoat

The *Vicar*, *Churchwardens and Parochial Church Council*

request the pleasure of the presence of

.... Mrs Fountain Family ....

at a

SERVICE OF THANKSGIVING

FOR THE COMPLETION OF THE CHURCH AND
DEDICATION OF THE NEW WEST END

by the LORD BISHOP OF CARLISLE
(The Right Reverend Cyril Bulley, M.A.)

On *FRIDAY, 15th SEPTEMBER, 1967 at 7-30 p.m.*

Clergy will Robe
in St. Paul's School.

R.S.V.P. by 8th September to
Mr. H. Hayhurst,
9, Grantley Road,
Barrow-in-Furness,
Lancs.

Refreshments in St. Paul's School following the Service

Handing the key of the new extension to the Bishop.
From left to right: The Bishop of Carlisle, Bishop Bulley; Raymond Fountain, Vicar; Archdeacon Richard Hare; Charles McWilliam (head of the building firm).

there to hand to the Bishop the new key, and some of the builders also attended. The choir anthems and the rousing singing of hymns such as 'Christ is made the sure Foundation' as the company processed up the aisle, must have shaken the new rafters, and as we left to meet in the church hall, everyone was fairly glowing with joy at this completion at last achieved.

We had a further dedication by Bishop Russell White to consecrate a new side chapel with a lovely altar made in the Robert Thompson Workshop in Kilburn. Raymond furnished the chapel with a carpet and a Service book in memory of his parents, and as a thanks offering for the joys experienced at St. Paul's, Barrow.

When Victor Harper had served his two years and had been ordained Priest he was appointed to a Lakeland parish as Vicar. Raymond then found himself without a colleague at St. Paul's for over a year, and though he no longer had the responsibility of St. Aiden's, he was getting ever more busy with committees and was also an inspector of schools as well as attending the Mayor's engagements from time to time. Lay volunteers helped with youth activities but Raymond took the Sunday evening meetings and confirmation classes, and of course the baptism and wedding talks.

A great friend, Miss Butler, who was elderly but had often spent time with the children, sometimes taking them to Walney beach, asked me if she thought the Vicar would be happy to have a holiday at her expense with the children, as she knew a lovely beach they would enjoy in North Wales. She was off there shortly for a holiday and we could join her when convenient. Miss Butler was concerned at how tired Raymond was looking. We were thrilled at this offer, but had no idea how thrilling the holiday was to be, until we got to North Wales and found we were booked in the Portmerion Hotel. We had two bedrooms and a bathroom at the end of a passage, with a door that was all mirror, so no one was heard passing our rooms even. We were told it was the suite that Noel Coward booked to write one of his plays. That was the holiday of a lifetime, and the girls were as pleased as we were to be invited again in the summer holidays. We had the terriers with us and they certainly enjoyed good fare, and our meals were the most delicious we had ever enjoyed.

Soon after our return Raymond had the help of a new curate, the Reverend Peter Mosley, and his wife Shelagh, who had two small daughters, Hilary and Nicola. Peter arrived a bit undecided as to whether the Ministry was really his calling, as it did impose financial strain on family.

Extension Financing Completion Plans

Soon after our return from holiday, Dr. Allan decided it was time for Mother Fountain to settle in hospital as she was no longer taking food or drink. She was not unhappy about this as she spent much time asleep and only occasionally could she recognise Raymond and, as these times became more rare, she finally died peacefully in her sleep.

Sara meanwhile was leaving St. Paul's school, and had decided to end school with a party for her whole form at the Vicarage. When told that forty children were coming to the party I had a word with the headmaster, asking if he could spare the time to help run a party for his top class. He was very amused to hear Sara wanted the whole class at a farewell party. He readily agreed to help and said his wife would come along too. Raymond at once started to think up clues for a treasure hunt all round the garden as a final game, so that they could find treasure just before they left. A friend in Grange, who ran an art shop, agreed to make up forty pencils and india rubbers having the names of all forty children. We went looking for cheap 'costume jewellery' gifts for girls; we got lots of chocolate coins, small cars or oddments to try to suitably fill an old trunk which looked like a treasure chest and could be buried under plenty of straw in the garden. I had a busy time preparing simple food to be placed in the kitchen, the hall, the dining room and the sitting room. Each 'set out' was labelled by the colour of the form sports teams, to have ten pupils in each room with a team captain in charge to ensure that all had a fair share of food and drink. The Bundys organized team games before tea and after came the great treasure hunt. All went very happily and it was fun to watch the excitement when the treasure chest was found. Though very simple gifts, all seemed to enjoy their treasure, and queued up to say farewell to Sara and wish her well at St. Anne's School as they were wished happy times at their new schools.

Elizabeth welcomed home after her first term as a boarder at St. Anne's School, Windermere.

One of the very attractive features of the new church extension, were the large, glazed, west entrance doors framed in oak, etched with pictures depicting St. Paul and maps of his Mediterranean journeys, and which allowed a view of the church interior. There was great dismay when the local post office engineers arrived and placed two telephone boxes on the pavement, hiding these doors.

Raymond requested to the postmaster to kindly have these removed to the previous site a little way up the road, where one had been sited before being replaced by these two boxes. This request was refused as being too costly, so Raymond enlisted the sympathy of the local MP who took up the request with the Postmaster General, and the telephone boxes were at once removed back to the original site, and all were very grateful to the MP for his prompt action.

The four hundred seats now in St. Paul's were filled almost immediately and the extension fund grew steadily to the target of £29,500. The new extension had ambulatories each side of the addition to the nave, offering space for more seating when needed, and a spacious entrance porch for notices, book racks, or for morning coffee and socialising after services. The additional space was needed when the local Flower Guild had a Flower Festival in St. Paul's in aid of the building fund.

It was decided to make it a Flower and Music Festival. Unfortunately the PCC did not give due recognition to a Music Festival being the responsibility of the Organist and Choirmistress, Miss Taylor, who had had responsibility for the music in St. Paul's for almost fifty years. When Miss Taylor was told that the boys' Grammar School choir was to take precedence over the Church choir as they were being asked to close the Music Evening with their contribution, Miss Taylor felt slighted and very sad that her choir, who sang every week and had given so much to the worship, were to be made to leave the church as soon as they had made their contribution, to make room for the School choir, who were to round off the evening.

Miss Taylor felt this a criticism of her choir as not being up to the task, and that she was getting too old to do justice to the occasion. She was grieved and unhappy, and reluctantly had to allow for a schoolmaster to practice at the organ and with his boys. It was decided without asking her permission. If her choir had performed last and they had had to leave the church last, that would have been easier to accept, but after all her contribution to the Worship in St. Paul's she felt she was no longer considered good enough, though of course the PCC had not considered this as a slight on the church choir performance. I felt Miss Taylor's grief very deeply, as I knew she shed many tears over this arrangement. To try to ease the situation a little Raymond and I felt the Church choir had deserved a good party to wind down after their session, and they all responded with enthusiasm to the idea of coming straight to the Vicarage for a party, (men and boys) to thank them for all the work they put into this effort. I was sad I could not persuade Miss Taylor to look in, but she was never a socialiser. Great friends though we were, and had many an outing together, only once in our eleven years in the parish did I get her to drop in for a morning coffee, and then she came as her friend wanted to come with her to coffee.

Margaret Taylor's choir at St. Paul's, Barrow-in-Furness.

The Flower Guild did a wonderful display and much money was raised by huge attendances over three days. The choir sang their hearts out, and we could never forget the lovely singing by four little lads on the chancel step singing 'Let the bright seraphim', their treble voices soaring to the roof, and heard so clearly throughout the church. Margaret's playing of Mozart's inspired 2nd movement of the Clarinet concerto I felt expressed her sadness, as she played that haunting music with such tender feeling. We never heard it after without being reminded of that lovely evening of flowers and music, and the joy of the building work completed to house so large an attendance in comfort.

The Vicarage buffet and drinks party went very well with the choirmen there to assist with the excited boys. I guided the lads to the dining room for their food and Coke, and the men had their provisions in the sitting room. A very small boy with a studious look behind owlish specs said he would like to join the men as he preferred the 'hard stuff' to 'coke'. A choirman overhearing this chased him back to the dining room. Raymond, having stayed to thank the other choir, later came to thank our choir for all the practice and effort they had given to their great performance.

We went to see Margaret the next morning, and she was in her usual cheerful mood and laughingly told us of the excited way the boys had spent some time telling her of all the lovely eats at the party, and she shooed them out after a very short practice telling them she didn't want them ill, after the previous evenings indulgence. I was later told I had missed a treat by not staying to hear the Grammar School choir. I was well satisfied with the music I had heard, but glad the boys' contribution went well and hoped they had had a party arranged. After all the effort and excitement of such an occasion a party provides a wind-down before bed.

August 1969: Unwanted Decision Problem Arises

• •

I suppose that after eleven great years at St. Paul's it should not have come as a great surprise that Simeon Trustees should think it time to offer Raymond a move. Raymond was asked to consider moving to All Saint's Church, Faringdon, then in Berkshire (soon to be Oxfordshire). Raymond was not wanting a move but was urged this was a parish to consider, so he went to visit Faringdon. He returned satisfied it was not for him, and told the Trustees. He was then twice urged to reconsider. Raymond tried to get in touch with Bishop Bulley, but the Bishop was on holiday in the Isle of Man. The pressure from the trustees gave Raymond the idea that maybe St.

Paul's was wanting a younger clergyman, as Raymond was now in his late 50s. Having decided to accept this living, I spent a day with Raymond in Faringdon. The Vicarage looked imposing Georgian from the outside, but inside was a shock. A moth-eaten covered door led from the front porch into the house. A long dark passage led to the back of the house. The front sitting room could be divided by a folding wooden screen, but the screen was in the damp large cellars extending under the whole house in various rooms. Another moth-eaten baize covered door shut off the cellars near the front staircase, which had attractive bannisters. The dining room at the back of the house looked rather Tudor and was an attractive room but for having a door leading into a passage to the back door past stables. Another door led into a little utility room with large hooks from the beams, where meat may once have been hung. The kitchen was opposite the utility room, and a back staircase between them. These stairs led to a bathroom, a small and a very large bedroom with doors each end, leading either to back or front stairs. There were three other bedrooms near the front stairs and stairs up to three attics. The whole house needed redecorating, and the bare floors in many rooms had gaps and holes between the floor boards.

Faringdon Town was attractive, with a rather Cotswold look, surrounded by pleasant country views. The daughter church in the village of Little Coxwell was built in the reign of Elizabeth I, and was a delight. Faringdon Church had been a monastic foundation, but the monks moved to Beaulieu. The nave was about the same length as the large chancel, and the sanctuary also large. The organ and choir was at the west end, rather than in the chancel; the sound was not good from the chancel as a large central tower trapped the sound. A lovely old church but in need of a facelift inside. We were told they had a good organist and choir.

The church wardens, Cecil Blissett and John Bolter and the Secretary of the PCC took us to the Vicarage and we sat in the rather shabby large front room to discuss how the Vicarage could be improved, and the needs of the church and parish. Peggy Spinage, the PCC Secretary, was very helpful and business-like and said the

Vicarage would be redecorated, and I could advise colours and other necessary improvements. They had decided to have oil-fired heating in the Vicarage as it was a very cold old house in winter. (Mr. Heber-Percy, the Lord of the Manor next door, always brought a large rug with him when he attended meetings in the Vicarage which had once been the Dower House, for widows of the gentry living in Faringdon House). Faringdon House had been the home of Lord Berners and was left to Robert Heber-Percy in his will. Much of the property in Faringdon was owned by the Lord of the Manor and Robert Heber-Percy was known to be very kind to all his tenants.

Raymond's encouragement in accepting the living was that his predecessor, Canon Roberts, was known as a most inspiring Vicar who had helped many young men to offer for the Ministry, so Raymond felt good foundations would have been laid during Canon Roberts' time in Faringdon.

Journeying home, though we could not complain of the kindly welcome we had received, neither of us felt happy that Faringdon was the right parish, but events seemed to have decided we must take it on. We wondered how we were going to furnish so large a Vicarage, and find the money for the carpets and curtains needed. A very neglected garden was a bit daunting also. It was a sizeable area, beautifully walled in alongside the very orderly grounds of Faringdon House. The lawn would need scything for a start as the grass was very long. A vegetable section below the lawn was sporting a great variety of fine weeds. Reluctantly Raymond informed the Bishop of our proposed move. The Bishop said that as Raymond had booked him to preach on St. Paul's Day at the end of January, he wanted Raymond to remain at St. Paul's until then. Faringdon was not too pleased as they hoped to have Raymond inducted before Christmas. We were pleased to have a last Christmas in Barrow.

In the autumn St. Paul's was told of the proposed move. The Churchwardens and Miss Taylor the organist also were the day before the announcement and she was in tears. She thought the Bishop should have made him assistant Bishop (not a role that would appeal to Raymond). After the announcement in church about our move, we were a little surprised that no one made any reference to the announcement as they left church. I was later told the congregation were so saddened and shocked they felt if they said anything they would all end in tears. Mr. Agar, a P.C.C. member, when told said he must sit down, he was so shocked. He went on to say that when he first knew Raymond he was sure he would do little for the church, he wouldn't have enough drive to get things done. We were amused but enjoyed the honest northerner's comments. The wife of the Mayor, Mrs. Gabbatt said she was quite heartbroken, she so wanted Raymond to be still here to take her funeral.

We now wished we could have known how St. Paul's congregation were to feel about Raymond's difficult decision to leave Barrow. We had to accept that this may have meant it was God's will that we should move in, and it is perhaps better go while one's ministry is appreciated, rather than stay on until one's congregation was praying for one to move on. It was not going to be easy to leave our lovely new Vicarage which had become very much the home of the parish, and full of wonderful memories. The watchnight service on December 31st was well attended and I'm sure all of us were wondering a little anxiously what the new year offered us all.

Descent from the Mountain Top

A week later, the girls were back at St. Anne's School, Windermere. At the Vicarage we had non-stop callers, anxious to be of any help, and many came with invitations to have final meals with them. We received an invitation from Bishop Bulley to lunch with him at Rose Castle, but at the same time Raymond was asked if he would go to Hildenborough to take a memorial service for Doctor Davison who had just died. Raymond agreed to do this as the Davison's had been such good friends during our time in that parish. We also were aroused one morning about 6am. to ask if Raymond would go to help with the exorcism of a Priest thought to be in the grip of a demonic depression.

Raymond returned after we had lunched just in time to take a 2pm funeral. An Ulverston clergyman took the sad clergyman back to live at their Vicarage for a time.

Despite a bitterly cold evening our faithful prayer group all turned up. Mrs. Scarlin, Miss Knight, Kath Horton and Mr. and Mrs. Boardman, Mr. Webb, Cathie Hamilton, Horace Hayhurst Pauline Spencer, Mr. Price and his sister, Mrs. Clare, Miss Balance, Mrs. Everett and Miss Child. The study of a passage in 2 Kings about the putting up and pulling down hill shrines caused some quiet amusement, and we ended as usual with prayers followed by cups of tea and chat. When all left at about 10pm we were ready for bed.

We had a fairly sleepless night having had a phone call from Faringdon to say the Churchwardens were coming up to see us at the weekend as things had changed a little but they hoped it would not put Raymond off coming. We were left wondering whatever the change could be, and Raymond thought to change our mind at this late stage would not only worry Faringdon, but would also unsettle Barrow, who had just become resigned to a change of Vicar and was already interviewing some interested in the Parish.

Cecil Blissett and John Bolter, the Faringdon Churchwardens, turned up at Matins on Sunday morning. As they left the church with us, they were not made to feel very welcome, and some exclaimed, "We hate you," while others asked, "Haven't you got any decent clergy in the south that you have to come and take ours?" All a bit embarrassing, but Cecil and John were amused at the banter, and not worried since Raymond had accepted their parish already.

No doubt they really had come to see what Barrow thought of Raymond as a Vicar, as they said they wanted to let Raymond know that having told him he could have a curate in Faringdon, they now decided they couldn't afford one. Going to a large Vicarage on less income, and with more work, Raymond taking on two churches single-handedly and being eleven years older than when we went to Barrow was more convincing that this really was not right for Faringdon nor for Raymond. Why did the Patrons feel it was so right we wondered, but it was too late to change now. We were glad to be told the house is central heating was now in order. Knowing that that bit of England could be pretty cold unlike Barrow where we had a generally mild climate thanks to the gulf stream, we would appreciate the heating. In St. Paul's Vicarage we had one night store heater on the landing and one in the hall and kitchen and dining room, and a coal fire in the sitting room, which was adequate heating. We did wonder how much of the heating we would be able to afford in Faringdon as oil fired heating would be a lot more expensive, and the heating of the large rooms could be costly. Inevitably the sad day came when our lovely new Vicarage had to be stripped of all of our belongings and left ready for some lucky new Vicar, who we hoped would be as happy as we had been.

After a pretty tiring morning, we saw the furniture vans set off for Faringdon on 20th January. We were to follow on and see the furniture in, and were to go to Hildenborough for Raymond to take the funeral of Doctor Davison, before returning to St. Paul's for Raymond's farewell Sunday on 25th January, St. Paul's Day, when Bishop Bulley was coming to preach and to say farewell to us and no doubt to have a word with the Wardens about finding a Vicar to succeed Raymond. We were glad the girls were allowed to take time out of school to see Faringdon and to attend the Induction of Raymond as Vicar. When leaving Hildenborough we were to collect the girls from Windermere and they were invited to stay with the Haleys for the weekend. We would stay in a small hotel in the parish. Before we set off after the furniture van Norma, our artist tutor, took us home for a coffee. It was sad saying goodbye to Norma but she seemed serious about a move south somewhere near us, so planned to visit when we had settled in. A very cheering thought.

Arriving in Faringdon we called on the Blissetts to tell them of our plans, and they said they were expecting us to an evening meal. Nancy was known for her excellent catering, and gave us a superb meal. We slept at the Bell Hotel, very near the Vicarage. The next day we were able to get away about midday, having just seen the furniture in before driving to Tunbridge Wells, where Mary Hicks was to put us up for the night before going to Hildenborough for Dr.

Davison's funeral. It was good to see many old friends and we were pleased to hear many were coming to Faringdon to Raymond's Induction. We got back late to Faringdon and again had a night at the hotel.

We were roused early by the church clock playing a hymn on the bells, which it did every three hours, with different hymns for each day. (It had amused me by playing 'God moves in a mysterious way' while we were moving in. I felt I could say Amen to that.) We made an early start back to Barrow, and called for the girls in Windermere at 2.15pm. We went to the Barrow station café for fish and chips for auld times sake. A popular treat for the girls and Richard Haley.

On our way to the Haleys we stopped at the home of Muriel Railton, a favourite teacher at St. Paul's School and a good friend. Muriel gave us tea and we agreed we would always keep in touch. We left the Haleys quite quickly after delivering the girls as they realised we were tired after our long day. We were soon settled in the East Mount Hotel on Abbey Road, and even a noisy Scout affair there did not prevent us quickly getting off to sleep. Raymond was first off getting the car from the Vicarage garage. After a good breakfast Raymond went to take the 8am and 9am services. Elisabeth and Sara joined me at the 9am service looking smart in their St. Anne's school blue greatcoats and berets.

Sid Bundy, St. Paul's headmaster and churchwarden Horace Hayhurst greeted us very warmly as we went in and Norma took us off to her home after service for coffee before Matins, when Raymond was to preach his final sermon as Vicar. At the evening service Bishop Bulley preached. He said how shocked he was and saddened to hear on his return from holiday that Raymond was to leave the diocese. He spoke of the great strides St. Paul's had made in recent years, not only the completion of the church building, and the Hall so well converted from the old school, the completion of the new school and the building of the new Vicarage but, perhaps best of all, the building up of the congregation, the youth work and the deepening of Spiritual life and Fellowship.

Mine was not the only aching heart as the wonderful choir sang so movingly the anthem, 'How beautiful are the feet of those who preach the Gospel of Peace.' The choirstalls were almost overflowing and they certainly sang from the heart. Some former choirmen returned to sing this special evening. For us the overriding emotion was of gratitude to God for all that we had gained in that Christian family. Many tears flowed in the farewells that followed.

Raymond thanked George Higham for having been such a support as his Churchwarden all through our eleven years with them, and we again thanked them for all the hospitality they had given us over the years, and not least for the excellent lunch they had given us between services on this, our last day. Pat and George had become real friends and it was hard to leave them.

The Haleys came and shepherded us to the door and took us of to their house for a light supper. We returned the girls to school and, after a night in Barrow, we decided to spend the next two nights in The Grange Hotel, Grange-over-Sands, before collecting the girls to travel to Faringdon with us. We went back to Barrow the next day to see Mrs. Anderson, my wonderful help in our last few years, now cleaning up the Vicarage. We persuaded her to join us in sitting on upturned kitchen drawers, to eat pork pies with us, as lunch. We were caught in the act by Mr. Hayhurst, who was amused to see us lunching together in this way. We called on Mrs. Preston who had been so kind to Raymond's mother when she became housebound, often visiting her or sitting with her if we had to be out together.

We went on to St. Paul's to have a last look at the church and found Miss Taylor there, so were able to thank her for all the years she had given to the music of St. Paul's, and especially the music and large choir at our final service. We assured her we would be up to see her as often as we could manage. We then took ourselves for a quiet reflective walk along Walney beach, which seemed to bristle with so many happy memories of the babes playing there when very young and, as they grew, the fun we had taking our dogs for long walks. It also had one very sad memory of having a greatly loved Jack Russell bitch, Buzzy, shot when she was only a year old, by a mentally retarded young man, who was known to shoot anything that moved. A great heartbreak.

On returning to the Grange Hotel I had a phone call from Mother in Bournemouth to say that she had decided to attend the Induction in Faringdon, and Aunt Grett also hoped to be there. This was cheering news. Rather worrying news was that my nephew Stewart Hall whom I scarcely knew, having last seen him as a little boy, was now living in the Isle of Wight and was considering a move to find work on the mainland. He was working long hours and felt that leaving his wife Kit, for long days to look after their two little daughters was a bit of a strain on their marriage. He wondered if we could put up his wife and children for a week or two. I reminded Mum we had only moved in the furniture, but we could accommodate them when we were unpacked.

The next day we collected our menagerie which we had boarded nearby when leaving the Vicarage. With our luggage and finding room for the girls and theirs it was quite difficult to get Jet, Topsy and Towser comfortably in for quite a long run. Goofey travelled in a rabbit cage, with Jet lying on top, and the terriers in the back with the girls.

I persuaded Raymond to let me revisit the Vicarage garden to drop a few blossoms on the graves of Dusk and Buzz, buried in the garden and on the grave of Norma Ingrams' lovely Alsatian/Ridgeback cross who also was at rest in our garden. I felt their spirits would follow us. After all, in Revelation, in St. John's vision, there were lots of living creatures round the throne of God, and Christ seen riding on a 'White horse' which gives hope that we shall again see our friends of the animal kingdom after this life.

Elisabeth and Sara were happy to get out of school to see Faringdon and we were all thankful to arrive safely around 7pm. Having a walled-in garden, the dogs were left to explore it while we did some necessary unpacking, and while Elisabeth and Sara managed to make a meal. The Blissetts looked in and Brenda gave nice vases to the girls as a welcome present each.

Faringdon

All Saints Church, Faringdon

January 1970

• •

Raymond's Induction to All Saint's Church was to be on Saturday, 31st January. That gave us one day to gather in friends and relatives, to unpack and get bedrooms ready. Elisabeth and Sara, full of energy, were up early shopping, then serving coffee for people calling to introduce themselves and bid us welcome. In between they worked on unpacking kitchen essentials.

I was delighted to see the Vicarage 'Help', Mrs. Belcher, turn up, ready to tackle anything. Having worked at the Vicarage for some years, she was not perturbed by the constant interruptions and the rushed pace at which we all had to work. Mrs. Belcher always managed to take it all in her stride, and was amazingly quick in getting the bedrooms ready for guests, and packaging and boxes all stowed away. I never did see Mrs. Belcher anything but cheerful though, like the rest of us, she had had plenty of ups and downs in life. She was a member of Underiver Church, a nearby village, and was a true Christian, always out to help others in any way she could.

Raymond managed to drive over to Bournemouth and back, collecting Mother and Aunt Gretta, and all arrived in time for lunch. My sisters Cara and Jill turned up with a family friend of long standing, Flo Vaughan, just in time to join us at lunch.

They were very quick to help to get the chaos sorted and to create a welcoming home. A cousin of Raymond's turned up from Sussex during the afternoon. Joyce was a school teacher at Lewes Grammar School, so quickly settled to helping Raymond in his study, getting his books unpacked and into bookcases in the right order to be ready for him to refer to for preparing Sunday sermons. By evening the house looked homely and Raymond's library very orderly and inviting.

We decided to call it a day and, now all was quiet, have our evening meal. The church wardens called in to ask Raymond to join them in church for a rehearsal of the Induction procedure. Having been fed, Elisabeth and Sara were first to get off to bed in the large room overlooking the churchyard. When we went up to bed at midnight we first looked in to see the girls who were still awake and chatting.

"O Daddy do look and see if the headless ghost is in the churchyard," said Sara. "We were told a headless ghost is seen to walk round the churchyard at midnight sometimes. He had his head blown off in the Civil War, by a cannon ball. The cannon ball is still lodged in the church tower wall."

As far as we could see no one was in the churchyard.

Progress started a little slowly the next morning, not only because of weariness, but the lights had all fused. Having got that sorted out as soon as we had finished breakfast, a tramp called in search of food which gave our new home a genuine Vicarage feel. He was sent on his way well fed. That was the start of the bell ringing as visitors from Barrow, as well as locals kept dropping in to see our new set-up. Again, Elisabeth and Sara did a lot of showing folk the house and providing them with coffee and biscuits.

We were all delighted to welcome once more Bishop Russell-White and his wife from Tonbridge. The Bishop was coming to represent the Simeon Trust Patrons of Faringdon, and to present Raymond to the church and parish. There was a bit of reminiscing over Hildenborough days, and Raymond then took them to have lunch in the nearby Bell Hotel, which gave him a bit of much needed relaxation before the service and after meetings.

Ken Bradley and his wife Margaret turned up just after lunch and had driven down to be able to drive the girls back to school. Ken Bradley, his wife, Margaret and daughters, Elizabeth and Janet, had moved to Barrow from Cheshire, and the girls attended St. Paul's School, as did Elisabeth and Sara. Elisabeth and Elizabeth Bradley were in the same form and quickly formed a lasting friendship. Ken became the lay reader, ever willing to help Raymond, and Margaret helped a lot with church activities. Ken came with a message from the many at St. Paul's unable to travel down for Raymond's Induction, to tell Raymond that they were all going to spend time in St. Paul's Church, praying for him during the time of the Induction service in Faringdon. This wonderful prayer support was certainly felt during an inspired service, with a full congregation (a coach load also came from Barrow).

I was delighted to see Mrs. Chavasse, (now widow of Bishop Chavasse) had also come to the service, as she lived in Oxford. I wondered if she had travelled in with the Bishop of Oxford, Harry Carpenter, who was to preach at the service. Raymond had not previously met Harry Carpenter, but the sermon revealed that he knew a lot about Raymond's previous ministries. He was so fulsome in praise of Raymond it was a bit embarrassing, and I felt that Mrs. Chavasse having known Raymond from his student days and in Hildenborough, had been talking of Raymond on her way to Faringdon. Mrs. Chavasse said to me as she was leaving, that she had heard many good sermons by Harry, but that was the best she had ever heard.

We were told all were invited to our welcome meeting at the home of the peoples' warden, John Bolter and his wife Judy, at a nearby farm. The Bolters had a wonderful feast spread out to greet us which rivalled the famous hospitality of the Northerners. All our Barrovian friends were very impressed with this greeting to their new Vicar and felt it a very happy start for us. Gwyneth Tiarks used to tell me, "You will find most days very long in Vicarage life, but remind yourself all long days do come to an end. This had been a long day but with a very enjoyable end.

A feeling of anticlimax set in at the start of Sunday morning having to see Elisabeth and Sara loading up into the Bradleys' car for an early start on the long journey to Windermere, and then to Barrow for the Bradleys. Then the tender farewell to the coach party as we waved our St. Paul's family also off early, then a rush to be ready for the 8am service. There was a good attendance and at Matins, when Raymond 'read himself in' instead of a sermon, reading half of the 39 articles, we were given a warm welcome as people left.

It was sad to see Raymond alone in the very long chancel, after seeing him with the St. Paul's choirmen and boys, but the large square tower in the centre of the church meant poor acoustics and the organist and choir sat at the west end of the nave.

St. Mary's,
Little Coxwell

The daughter church, St. Mary's Little Coxwell, was set in a pretty village, and had been in use since the reign of Elizabeth I. A most attractive church set in lovely country. The Vicar's warden, George Eyre-Brook, and his wife, Diana, were most welcoming. George had a farm, and they had a son and daughter. We were at once invited to have a meal with them, the first of many as they became good friends and were most hospitable

After Evensong at All Saints, Nancy and Cecil spent the evening with us in the Vicarage. They left fairly early having arranged with Raymond that Cecil and John Bolter would drop in for coffee after early service the next morning for Parish talk.

Getting To Know You

On leaving the church on Monday after the early service, I walked out with one of those attending the service. Giving a rather critical look at the church interior I was unwise enough to remark that the church could do with a good spring clean. This was certainly true.

The furnishings, seat cushions and kneelers had a well worn look, the windows were in need of cleaning, there were large paper notices tied round ancient pillars. To me it had a sad look after the comparatively modern, light and very polished St. Paul's. Even the church lighting was poor, and strings had been tied from one light to the next, in an effort to improve the lighting over the pews. The Faringdonian I spoke to was offended and told me brusquely, "We *love* our old church, dust and all." Trust me to start off on the wrong foot!

Over coffee in the Vicarage, Raymond was told by Cecil and John of the church officers, elderly and housebound who eagerly awaited a visit from the Vicar after a long interregnum. Cecil ran a local grocery business, and being on the local council knew many Faringdon residents and was most helpful. Raymond said how grateful we were to the Secretary of the P.C.C. who had been so helpful in the redecorating of the Vicarage, and it certainly was very different from our first view of the house, and the newly installed heating much appreciated in January.

I was having a chat with Nancy Blissett in the kitchen and told her of my nephew and family who intending to come for a stay any time now. Nancy at once offered to introduce Kit and children to other young families and to help her get the children attending a school while with us. Though Raymond was very quickly down to work, I was still not quite unpacked and ready, when Stewart rang to tell us they were on their way to Faringdon.

As it was then late evening and we had had a busy day, as I was still getting friendly callers coming to welcome us, and Raymond was out much of the day. I suggested to Raymond that he should get to bed and I would see my nephew and family in and fed and settled. They finally arrived at 12.30am having had some job in finding their way late at night in a strange area. They were quickly refreshed and settled and we were all abed by 2am. Raymond was relieved he had settled early. I spent much of the day getting to know Stewart, who I'd last seen when he was very young, and it was my first meeting with the family, his wife, Kit and daughters Susie-Ann and Jacquie. Two delightful little girls very pleased to have the dogs to play with, our border collie, Jet, and Jack Russells, Topsy and Towser. Kit was pleased I had a lot of Elisabeth and Sara's clothes put aside for giving to a charity shop as Kit was a good needle worker, and able to adjust many things for her two. Nancy Blissett quickly had the family to a meal and soon had helped Kit to get the children entered into the local school.

Though Stewart had to get back to work, he came at weekends and was able to meet up with his Dad who came to meet the granddaughters. Stewart had been born while my brother Bill, his dad, was in the army in Africa for five years. When Bill returned home Stewart was four years-old. Bill's marriage had broken up during his long years abroad. Though Bill had corresponded and sent maintenance for Stewart they had rarely met, Bill having remarried and Stewart having had little contact with him as a babe. They got on very happily and it was a great joy to Bill to be able to get to know the family, even though belatedly.

Stewart was glad Raymond readily agreed to baptise the girls and Stewart also, as he had not been baptised, and before they left us Stewart and Kit were confirmed together when Elisabeth was confirmed in Oxford Cathedral.

I enjoyed having Kit and children with us until early March. In that month Stewart joined us most weekends. Susie was not very happy at a strange school, but stuck it bravely. Kit was a help to me around the house and with meals when I was out visiting with Raymond. In February I travelled up North and had a weekend with Norma Ingram, to spend time with Elisabeth and Sara who were staying with a school friend in Roose for half-term break. Mrs. Tusan returned the girls back to school as I had to get back to Faringdon. I looked forward to getting the girls back with us when we could find a school which could offer them a place.

It was cheering to find Raymond at Oxford station. As we drove home he admitted he felt depressed about having accepted Faringdon under pressure from the patrons as he didn't feel it was the right parish but, having accepted it, must do the best he could.

The evening meditation and prayer group was well attended and cheered us on, and the Blissetts spent a short time with us in the Vicarage after the service.

A visit to Mrs. Chavasse in Oxford the next morning was enjoyable and we were greeted like long-lost friends. After lunch Mr. Eyre-Brook took us round Little Coxwell village introducing us to many of the parishioners. The Lord of the Manor, Mr. Berners, made us very welcome and we stayed to tea with him. A very charming gentleman in delightful house and surroundings.

Stewart, Kit and family left to return to the Isle of Wight. Stewart having decided to try life in catering on a liner bound for Australia. What he saw of Australia decided him to make their home there. Before setting off they brought their new son Michael to be baptised. In time his widowed mother joined them there and kept us in touch with news of the family.

When Stewart had told his mother of their intention to settle in Australia, he was delighted that she invited his father to spend the weekend with her and her husband so that Stewart and family could see his father and mother together, as he was too young to remember seeing his father return from Africa after the war. Bill went with them to Southampton to wave the family off to Australia – the last time Bill saw Enid and Stewart, though they had always remained good friends despite the early marriage breakdown. Stewart wrote to his Dad from Australia to send him photos of his enlarged family when they had achieved three daughters and three sons and were well settled, but his father died of cancer just shortly before the letter arrived. Enid sent us Christmas photos of the family; we found it amusing to see the family in bathing costume under the Christmas tree.

Settling Down to Work

· ·

Faringdon Town was of a different character from our previous two parishes. Now a different generation also was noticeable in church

Faringdon High Street

life. Faringdon had a long history, and had been mentioned in the Domesday Book. A pleasing town with a village like feel as it was surrounded by country of lovely views and fields inviting walks. All Saints Church had a fine peal of bells, which sounded out hymns during the day every two hours. On the day we were moving in it amused me that the clock kept telling 'God moves, in a mysterious way.' Sunday's tune was 'Holy, Holy, Holy.' When the clock one night continued the two-hourly hymn, a furious hotel owner rushed to the Vicarage abusing Raymond for having let the hymns ring out, preventing her guests from sleeping. The clock minder was summoned at once to put things right. One newcomer to Faringdon demanded that the bells should be silenced as he found them annoying, but the bells could not be silenced, and many visiting bellringers came to enjoy them to the annoyance of visitors who found the long evening of bell ringing quite intolerable. We found them enjoyable and they never disturbed our rest though we were in a bedroom overlooking the churchyard.

I had to get used to seeing little of Raymond most days; having no curate he found much to do round the two parishes. We did however make many friends quite quickly as our 'Open House' policy found lots of parishioners of both parishes happy to drop in when round the shops. It was quite usual to have folk in for coffee, and some would stay on for a snack lunch and others would make afternoon teatime calls, so I was never lonely and enjoyed these visits. Two Little Coxwell friends, Mary Bowley and Frances Winteringham, became close friends. I was astonished to be told my friendship with Frances had upset some, because she was a Roman Catholic. She had been recently widowed and needed company.

When walking down to Little Coxwell with terriers Topsy and Towser, Frances and I met under our umbrellas in heavy rain. Frances had her Jack Russells with her, Tipsy and Meg, and they really introduced us. We met again the next day having both been invited to tea with the Eyre-Brooks. That started a great friendship and Frances was often in the Vicarage from then on. Tipsy and Meg always were keen to join any tea party and would try desperately hard to get a share of one's tea. Frances told me that, when she was giving tea to a former hospital matron she had worked with at the Radcliffe Hospital, she went to the kitchen for more tea and found her guest standing at the mantelpiece eating her cake because the dogs, one each side, were jumping up to share the cake (we found it easiest to succumb and give them crumbs).

Having called at a house opposite the church and finding no one in, Raymond left his card. Miss Katie Johnston wrote us a note inviting us to tea if we didn't mind visiting an atheist. Katie became a close friend and Raymond persuaded her to type the Parish Magazine for him as she had a good typewriter and worked for the Oxford University Press. Maybe Raymond's monthly sermon in the magazine interested her as she joined a class Raymond ran on the Christian Faith. Some attended as Confirmation preparation and one attender asked Katie if she was to be confirmed. She looked astonished and said, "Oh no, all our family are atheists." I had a strong feeling she was the least atheist of them all.

The Hon. Mrs. Craven lived nearby in Wadley Manor, said to once have been owned by Elizabeth I's cousin, Sir Henry Unton, whose impressive tomb was in the Unton Chapel in All Saint's church Wadley Manor was a delight to visit. When Raymond took Mrs. Craven her monthly communion as she was an invalid, I went along to enjoy this Elizabethan Manor House. Mrs. Craven always sent lovely flowers to the church at Festivals and kept a great interest in All Saints.

Mary Bowley, who lived in Little Coxwell, was a musician – a pianist – and had dogs. She was delighted to know we had daughters who studied music, one who played the organ, and the other the violin, and that I also had dogs. Mary's dogs were Labrador type cross, Betsy and Bridie. Mary and dogs became regular visitors to the Vicarage as Mary was a rather lonely loner, and we walked dogs together when possible.

My great friend in Barrow, Norma, my painting tutor, was quick to come and stay with us, and when Mr. Blissett heard she was a professional artist, showed her a very old canvas of a coat-of-arms that had once hung in the church. It was stacked in a corner, covered in cobwebs, was in holes and very grimy. He had been told it should be burnt, as restoring it would cost a fortune. Cecil valued it as a part of the church history and wanted Norma's opinion of what could be done with it. Norma at once volunteered to restore it without charge. I was roped in to help and learnt a lot about restoration work. Within a week it was clean and repaired, and was in need of oiling to restore the dried-out paint.

For several months it was my daily job to wipe over the canvas to ensure the oil poured through the back of the canvas did not set in drips on the surface. This treatment restored the original bright colours. When finished the coat-of-arms was restored to its original place, high up over the arch over the entrance to the chancel, providing much needed colour against the stonework.

Norma was very taken with the Faringdon area and went home to sell her Barrow house. Mary Bowley was deciding to move away to be near her sisters and Norma bought Mary Bowley's pretty cottage in Little Coxwell, as it had an ideal annex in the garden which made a splendid studio where Norma was kept busy painting portraits. Norma was soon running evening painting classes for the local council. We were delighted to have her near at hand again; she was quickly accepted into the local community and well loved by all.

The restoration of the old coat of arms in the church aroused enthusiasm for giving an uplift to the church interior and furnishings. A 'Servant's Guild' was formed of those keen to tackle embroidered hassocks, and to raise funds with coffee mornings to renew pew seat runners. We all felt there was a need for some rearranging of furniture, as long pews were hiding the impressive and noteworthy marble tomb of the Untons. It was decided that the vestry which was blocking a view of the Unton chapel was now too small for the choir, so should be replaced by a larger one in the north-west Victorian part of the church.

When this was achieved the Unton memorials in the chapel were in full view. A very generous member of the congregation was impressed by the work going on and made a great improvement to the church by providing magnificent roof lighting. A spotlight was fixed to show up the Unton tomb and the font area (a light over the font often keeps the babe interested enough to prevent tears!) Red runners on the pews added colour, and a kind man fitted neat wire racks to hold Bibles and new prayer and hymn books donated by members of the church, many dedicated to the memory of past church members.

As the months went by, new tapestry kneelers were gradually appearing throughout the church, giving it a much needed look of being well cared for. I made it my job each day to see that the Bibles and hymn books were neatly set in the racks in front of each pew which added a neat and colourful touch to the view on entering the church. The wonderful flower displays by the flower ladies added the final touch and these drew many appreciative comments from visitors. Shortly afterwards the Unton tomb was regilded as a memorial to a church member's husband who had recently died, which really returned the tomb to its original splendour.

It came as a shock to discover, under the Pye Chapel Holy Table, flower vases, a trog and tools and a dead mouse in a trap. To most clergy and church members, the Holy Table is considered to be set aside for God's use, for the administration of the sacrament that is our memorial of Christ's great sacrifice. Raymond told the PCC he would arrange for a cupboard to be made in the North aisle where the flower ladies could keep their tools. They were not pleased and said they were sure God would not mind their use of the chapel altar. With some reluctance they used the cupboard, yet when visiting the church after our retirement I was sad to see the chapel altar again hiding these tools. One could only suppose to some it was their church in their generation and no longer looked upon as God's house.

When a church member planned to give a new pulpit to replace the large stone Victorian one, built when people sat in balconies, now removed, he hoped to give the church a wrought iron railed pulpit, so that those sitting in the north aisle would see the sanctuary, then hid by the overlarge tall pulpit. Alas, the Chancellor turned it down though it was approved by the PCC because he had received so many protests at the idea of moving the old stone pulpit. It was a great disappointment to the would be donor. PCC meetings could be acrimonious at times but all had wanted the offer of the new pulpit

Barbara Humphry, though a Quaker, came regularly to the early Communion Service and we met most days for silent prayer together, praying for a deeper, more loving Fellowship to grow in the church. It was an important start to the day for us and our friendship remained down the years though we rarely met after leaving Faringdon.

The Domestic Scene

In the Autumn of 1970, Elisabeth now 14 and Sara 12 years, were accepted in Headington School, Oxford, the only school locally which had vacancies. Even so they were not able to board until the January term, as girls sitting the Oxbridge exam stayed on until December. We could not have afforded the school fees, but to our delight we found the Headmistress was none other than a Bradford Cathedral member when teaching at Bradford Grammar School, was a great friend and had been at our wedding, where we had last met. When saying we did not think we could afford the school fees, Peggy Dunn assured us many girls gained scholarships and had support from several education charities. Peggy gave Raymond the addresses he could apply to and we received sufficient help for them to finish their school days at Headington.

As the girls were at home that first term, it helped them to make many Faringdon friends. The Organist's daughter's quickly became close friends as Ann and Jill Perkins were much the same and all shared the same interest in classical music. Much time was spent in each other's homes. Michael Perkins was a talented organist and had a well trained choir of men, women, boys and girls. Sir James Walker, a local squire, had founded as a memorial to his daughter Celia who had been a musician but tragically killed in a road accident when travelling abroad, a music fund for providing music concerts in church from time to time, and music competitions for promising young local musician students. These musical events were arranged and organised by Michael. A most enjoyable evening ended at the home of Sir James and Lady Walker over a buffet supper and offering a chance to talk with the musicians. A fair number of organ concerts were arranged, as Faringdon organ was a very good and modern pipe organ, a present to the church from a wealthy parishioner, and replaced a very poor instrument. These concerts attracted good attendances as did piano and choral concerts. They were also an encouragement to the many young music enthusiasts, and helped them gain confidence in playing in public. Michael allowed Elisabeth use of the organ in holidays for her practices, probably a valuable help in getting her later admission to a music college, since the organ which she was taught on in Oxford had little to commend it.

On two occasions while on holidays, once in Coniston and once in Bournemouth, we chanced to meet up with Michael and Pat Perkins with Ann and Jill and managed to spend some time together; the girls enjoyed one another's company on walks. It was after a

Above: Peter Brown, his wife Meg and their children.

Left: Susie-Ann and Jacqui just baptised in Faringdon Church.

holiday at a PCC meeting we learned that Faringdon could now afford a curate. An ordinand straight from Oakhill College, Peter Brown came for interview with his wife Meg. Meg was a clergy daughter so had some idea of what she was taking on. They had a small daughter, Katy, and a Labrador pup. Peter decided to accept the invitation to work with Raymond.

Peter's enthusiasm knew no bounds and he was brimfull of modern ideas on how to enliven church worship and attract more people into church life. I began to think Raymond was seen as his pupil; it was a long time since Raymond had been at theological college and Peter was keen to bring his ideas up to date. While appreciating his keenness and enthusiasm there were plenty in the congregation who could not accept Peter's ways. One gentleman at the early service was irritated when Peter assumed he had just joined the church, which he had in fact attended for years, and Peter's joy at seeing him in church and hoping he would come again really offended this parishioner. In morning prayer time, which Raymond and Peter shared each morning, Raymond tried to slow down Peter's enthusiasm that was putting off some of the congregation. Raymond came in chuckling when his talk with Peter resulted in Peter praying for Raymond to see the light and accept the need for moving with the times and start accepting new ways of worship.

When the PCC approved Raymond's arranging a mission to Faringdon by Wycliffe Hall students, Peter set to work on preparations, starting with sticking texts round the Vicarage while I was out. Poor Peter was requested to come and remove them! On leaving church on Sunday morning, I noticed there was some amusement as they passed Peter. As I left I noticed a sticker on Peter's stole. It read, 'I am a worm and no man.' I was quite sure this was not one Peter had adopted, or was even aware of. I rather suspected it might be choir as they would have been in the choir vestry before service.

The Mission kept everyone busy. Jim Hickenbotham, Principal of Wycliffe Hall, was a contemporary and good friend of Raymond's at Wycliffe and he had selected a good team of students. They went down very well in the parish while out visiting. Raymond started their day with Bible studies. His talks were much appreciated. Some told me they wished Raymond was on Wycliffe staff, they gained so much from the talks. Jim Hickenbotham spent his time in Faringdon with us. The students came in to lunch daily, provided by volunteer church members, who were kept busy in the kitchen. Breakfasts and teas were provided by the hostesses who kindly boarded them. We enjoyed a fair attendance at Mission meetings but mostly our church members. The students were discouraged by the poor response from the many folk they had visited. However, one young woman found great help from them. She was beginning to lose her sight and her husband had left her. She gained a very live Faith and to this day does a lot of work for the church.

The Invaders?

As our guest rooms were frequently used for family visiting, or visiting clergy coming to preach, and friends from our previous parishes, Elisabeth and Sara decided to take over attic rooms when they were home. The first night Elisabeth was in her attic, she came running down in the early hours, saying there was a noise like sawing wood in the next room.

I heard scuttering when I looked in and realised it was rats. There was an opening in the roof with a gutter running into the room. I had difficulty in persuading a rodent officer to come and investigate. He said the town did not get rats, it was probably birds. He did leave some rat poison food however. He came each day for five days and did find signs of rats. Meanwhile my Jack Russells, Topsy and Towser, were sure they heard rats in the walls and were very excited about this. To my horror they disappeared one morning through an opening in the attic and could be heard running between the walls. Eventually, to my relief, they re-emerged from the opening they had found and were as black as soot. A few days later there was the most offensive smell pervading most of the rooms, and Raymond and I slept on camp beds in his library for a few nights. Though friend Russell Spinage, one of the PCC (a builder and funeral director), came and had the floors up. No bodies were found. They could not take down walls so we had to wait for the smells to die down. Some months later I was taking a brush and dust pan around sweeping up hundreds of bluebottles, who presumably had taken the rat poison.

On our arrival at Faringdon, a former curate looked in to see us and said he had cut a fossilised rat off a beam in the house one time ! The Rodent Officer said a neighbour in Mr. Heber-Percy's grounds had made a hen run alongside the Vicarage wall, and that was what would have brought rats. They had promised to move the hen run. In our first week or two we had been troubled with flea bites, and were told stray cats had been allowed to use the downstairs rooms on chilly nights, as the then curate and family lived on the first floor, and the Vicar and his wife had used the attics. The downstairs was mostly used for meetings. Having dealt with that, the garden having been neglected during the interregnum, we wore gum boots in the garden until the long grass had been cut, as grass snakes and sometimes small patterned snakes were found sunbathing, possibly attracted by the lake in Robert Heber-Percy's garden next door.

We were also told of a ghost haunting the Vicarage. Ghosts were not a worry to us, but one lady calling at the Vicarage could not be persuaded to come into the house as the last time she did enter a lady dressed in white came through a closed door, bringing a very chilly feeling with her. A musician, who stayed a night with us when he came to give a concert in church, when asked if he slept well, replied that he had had a disturbed night. An unhappy spirit visited him and kept him awake, and he thought we should get someone to help to bring rest and peace to the poor soul. He said he detached himself from his mind and managed then to get to sleep.

Stewart and Kit's children said there were frightening noises in their bedroom. Not being worried by ghosts we rather dismissed these experiences, but we were also told of ghosts in the church. At an 8am Communion service a neighbour was trying to turn my

*Faringdon
Vicarage*

attention to something, but I couldn't see what was worrying her. After service she told me a gentleman in Elizabethan costume suddenly appeared and then vanished after listening to the five-minute sermon on 'Here we have no continuing city.' She was sure he was Sir Henry Unton illustrated in a history book we had. A lady coming in to coffee one morning said she had just been into church to collect a magazine, and there were three monks kneeling in the front pew at prayer. As she went towards them they vanished. The Church was originally a Monastic building, so maybe they revisited sometimes to pray with us.

When Elisabeth was at home for holidays, she used to do organ practice in the evenings, and she was sure there were people in the church with her, and she walked round to see if the flower arrangers were about. No one was with her, yet she felt there were people round the organ. She was not too easy about being in the dark church alone so I used to go in with her and enjoyed her practices. When my sister came in one evening with me, she asked if the man walking past the chancel was the verger. I told her I could see no one and the doors were all locked, so maybe it was one of the ghosts, but I never saw any. She hastily decided she was returning to the Vicarage.

Much more troublesome were vandals coming in, sometimes probably children, who delighted in throwing hassocks or books about. Sometimes they came in to have a smoke in a dark corner of the church. When we went in one morning to find deliberate desecration of the church, a new Bible on fire, the sanctuary carpets taken up and the cloth taken off the holy table, it seemed there had possibly been some black magic performance and the new vestry had been desecrated with foul messes. I had just opened the door of the church early morning when I had a powerful feeling of fear of going in. I was conscious of the hair on my neck rising. Michael Perkins was just arriving for some organ practice so we went in together. His wife very nobly tackled the cleaning up at once. Raymond got in touch with the Bishop to suggest he might come and reconsecrate the church, but was told it would be alright for Raymond to conduct the service. After the service there was a quite distinct change of atmosphere.

One morning Cecil Blissett came to ask me if I'd taken any books off the bookstall without my usual IOU note. as the account was £10 short. I had not had any books so he felt someone must have had a free book or two, as money in the wall safe could not be taken, unless a £10 note had not been posted in safely. A visit from the police shortly afterwards seemed to solve the problem as a boy they had caught thieving in a church had confessed to taking £10 from Faringdon wall safe. Having examined the safe, the policeman could hardly believe anyone could get at the money in that safe, so went off to question the lad about it. He was told that this lad saw Raymond leaving the church with a funeral party following the coffin, for a churchyard burial. The young man, aged nine years, went into the empty church through the wide flung doors, found the safe too safe, went into the vestry, found Raymond's big bunch of keys in his jacket pocket in the cupboard. He soon found the key he wanted, unlocked the safe and returned the bunch of keys to the pocket and was away before the Vicar was back. The policeman commented that that young man should have a bright future if his obvious abilities was properly channelled.

There were occasions when charity boxes at the back of the church were taken while a service was in progress, if no one was in the back pews. Police warned us that church doors must be locked if no one was on duty. Some churches had allowed very respectable looking elderly men into the church to look round, only to find too late that they were assessing the value of oak stools, silver and paintings or anything of value, which would be burgled for them in the night and packed and sent abroad by plane before the goods were missed.

It was decided to keep the church locked and anyone coming for the key to have a look round the church would be escorted – sad reflection on this money-mad age.

More of the Domestic Scene

By 1972 things seemed to be running more smoothly, though it was difficult to feel the church was really all pulling together since there always seemed to be times of discord about one matter or another, however congregations were keeping fairly steady and we had gained new members from the Methodist church when that church decided to join with the Congregational church in building a new church for them to share (the United Reform Church). The Congregational Church in the town was bought by the Roman Catholic Church, as they had been using a room in the Corn Exchange for services in Faringdon.

We sometimes had a clear day off and were able to drive over to Bournemouth with the family. My mother had had to go into hospital for some tests, and had unfortunately caught a cross infection and developed pneumonia. This left her frail and in need of nursing, so it was decided she should come to Faringdon to us for recuperation. After some weeks she was sufficiently improved to be able to return to Bournemouth for a holiday while we had a holiday in Cumbria. We exchanged Vicarages with our former curate of Barrow days. John Hancock did Sunday duty at Faringdon while Raymond did

Sunday duty in Coniston. A lovely holiday area we knew well. We met up with lots of old friends, and had wonderful fell walks and returned to Faringdon revitalised.

Mother returned and was happy to have had another spell at home, but realised she was not likely to return again as her heart was failing.

Parish and Vicarage entertaining seemed on the increase. I was asked if I would take over the Mother's Union, but home duties decided me I couldn't take this on. The number of members was very small and they were happy at the suggestion that they could meet with Littleworth M.U. who also had quite a small membership, and improve the meetings for both Mrs. Phipps, Vicar's wife was happy to have more members and this arrangement worked well.

Mr. Blissett came to see me to see if I could not make more visits to the town shops. He said the shops were upset I rarely was seen in their shops. Raymond liked to do the shopping to keep in touch with the shopkeepers, and learned the local news in this way, and there just was not enough money for us both to shop.

Not easy to explain this, but decimalisation had made all prices rise, and our income being much less than in Barrow, and with a more expensive Vicarage to run, lack of money was a real worry.

Seeing Raymond rather glooming when looking through the post, I asked, "More Bills?" "A bill for £70. Central heating oil, and we are already in the red." Going into church meeting my Quaker friend, Barbara, to spend time in silent prayer with her, which we tried to do each morning early, this bill featured in my prayers that morning and God had answered before I asked, it seemed. Raymond had been greatly cheered on opening a letter from the Inland Revenue, who were not usually so cheering, but they were returning a cheque for £70 because Raymond had over paid !

Generally we concentrated on praying for a greater and warmer Fellowship among the congregation, and for help in healing many divisions.

Some of the trouble was the introducing of new ideas about services and more modern gospel songs by Peter Brown. He had a very lively approach and did not want to continue with the book of Common Prayer and age-old hymns. I was not the only one who found this almost unbearably painful. After the joy of wartime services when one could drop into any church anywhere and find nothing changed in a fast changing mad world it was a tremendous loss to lose the unchanging world of the church.

It concerned Raymond that Little Coxwell congregation had taken to looking out of their doors to see which clergyman's car was outside the church, before deciding whether or not to attend. There were many complaints about the way services were changing.

Peter was very good with the young folk and helped the confirmation candidates to think seriously about the Faith. There was a sense of the confirmation being taken seriously. I was pleased the young girls decided to be old fashioned and they all dressed in white and wore veils because it was an important decision they were to make.

If a bride feels it an important occasion when taking life vows of commitment in marriage, is it not even more important when taking lifelong vows of commitment to serve God? If a child wins an award which is to be presented by the Queen or other Royal member, will they go dressed so casually as one is now required to do at a confirmation service. Dress up as you like for church, but best clothes to meet the Royals? I was cheered to see our little flock really dressed well for their confirmation. Sara was allowed home from school to attend the confirmation as she had had some weeks of preparation at school, so was allowed to be confirmed in her father's church. After service she got to know the Faringdon girls at the reception where they had a talk with the bishop over refreshments. The girls asked Raymond if they could have an evening first Communion with Sara as Sara could not get out of school in time for the 8am service. This service was well attended by congregation members who helped confirmands who had no relatives with them. It was a wonderful atmosphere and had a real family feel.

It was unfortunate that after a very busy and tiring weekend for Raymond, having entertained the Bishop and had much writing of confirmation cards, the register, cards for godparents, then the late service and the reception afterwards, a worthy member of the congregation chose to call early to see Raymond on Monday to take him to task for the 'poor preparation of the confirmation class, and then a miserable truncated service in the evenings.' This very unjust attack shocked Raymond and in no uncertain terms he exploded about all the quite unreasonable criticisms he came up against so often. We wondered if this person, so supportive as a rule, had even been to the service! Having fled in tears to complain to church wardens, Rural Dean, Archdeacon and Bishop, Raymond had visits from them all.   They came not to chastise, but to offer him their sympathy, having known of old the difficulties in Faringdon parish.

My mother was getting increasingly frail and meant that more of my time was taken up looking after her. When out and meeting church members some sympathised with me, having the added burden of looking after my Mother and not able to be at all the meetings. Though perhaps kindly meant, I told them this was no burden but a privilege to be able to return some of the care we had had lavished on us over the years. Mothers had a rough time during the war, worrying about us, and writing and constantly posting parcels, and in my case even tackling my washing of very soiled clothes when farming and not being able to get things washed. Mother would visit my farm whenever there was an opportunity, though sometimes travelling after dark when raids were overhead. Any help given now was well deserved.

While kept indoors I found relaxation practising oil painting to which Norma Ingram had introduced me to. Norma came one day and whipped away a painting of a cart horse and dog in a farm yard I'd scarcely finished. Sara wanted this, but it went to a charity show and was sold, to my amazement, and rather to Sara's disappointment.

Cecil and Nancy Blissett were sad when they heard we were to be away when their daughter Brenda was getting married, but fortunately a former Vicar of Faringdon who knew the family well was able to take the service.

Happily we were back from holiday for Raymond to take the

wedding of Elizabeth Eyre-Brook. A very pretty country wedding, with a family gathering for the reception in a large marquee on their lawn. The buffet was delicious as Diana Eyre-Brook was a first class caterer. The weather was cooperative and it was a most enjoyable occasion.

It was not unusual for clergy as well as Doctors to be prepared for night calls. Though at times it was calls from hospital or Nursing Homes to see very ill patients, or to baptise very frail new born babies. In Faringdon night bells often revealed a Police car lamp flashing, out on the front drive, and this was sometimes the Police having seen a light on in church, left by mistake by the last to leave the church. When I was woken by very persistent and heavy banging on the front door one night, after midnight, I looked out, but not seeing the usual police blue lamps flashing, I roused Raymond. While he got into a dressing gown I had put on trousers and a pullover in case needed to go out. We opened the door to find the young mother from next door, her elderly tenant who had an attic rented room, both in nighties and bare feet, shuddering and saying the gentlemen living with them had hanged himself in the garden! I was taken down to see if I could confirm he was dead. Raymond wisely went to the phone, to phone an ambulance, doctor, and police. Certainly the gent appeared to be dead, and then the elderly lady said she was in such pain, she couldn't move. Supposing she was having a heart attack, I found my way up to their bedrooms in the dark, and knowing the children would be there asleep, I managed to drag a blanket off the first bed, and took down some slippers. Having wrapped the elderly lady up in the blanket, and got her feet into someone's slippers, the Doctor arrived. He got her into the kitchen and I tried to make tea, but the gas was switched off. The ambulance arrived and the police, so I invited all into the Vicarage.

The young woman's parents arrived and collected the children and took them to their home. The rest stayed some time after the ambulance had removed the body from the garden. The Police having taken their notes, all had tea, and I was asked to keep an Alsatian pup for them for a few days, and they would return to collect it when they could.

It was about 4am when we shut the front door and returned to bed. I couldn't get to sleep, so was up to see Mrs. Belcher arrive to start the days work. I decided I would have another hour in bed, but the phone rang. My dear daughter, Elisabeth ringing up from school to say her form had a day off after exams, and were to visit White Horse Hill. As there were no conveniences up there she had invited the forty or so girls and teacher, to drop in to Faringdon Vicarage for tea. We had four loos so it was a good spot for tea!

The coach was impatiently waiting for Elisabeth, so I was not given a chance to reply. Raymond at once rang up the owner of the Boffin cafe in Shrivenham, who readily agreed to supply fifty tea scones. This lady had become quite a friend when she had learned that Raymond had spent his war as a chaplain in the R.A.F. in the Middle East. She had been in the W.A.A.F. and had received an award for having parachuted behind enemy lines on some dangerous exploit, or had had some such brave adventure. On hearing of the school girl invasion she at once volunteered to have a load of buttered scones ready for collection. Raymond then went and collected a great load of strawberries from the National Trust Old Barn, in Great Coxwell, where one of All Saint's members was custodian, and lived on that farm. A.B. Williams soon rustled up the strawberries, and was amused to hear of the crowd coming in the afternoon. 'A.B.' as he was always know often read the lessons in services, and was popular for the excellent reading in his fine voice, his reading making even the difficult passages more easily understood, as he was a good bible student.

At 3pm the coach rolled in, and Elisabeth noting we were not quite ready, handed the church key to the teacher suggesting they must take a look round the interesting old church first. Elisabeth and a friend helped us to finish culling the fruit, while I was busy filling lots of old margarine containers (kept for jellies at Sunday School parties). By 4pm. all were rushing back to the coach very pleased with the tea break, and some carrying tubs of fruit and cream back to friends unable to join the outing.

I should have realised this could be a dangerous precedence, because of course we were asked if it could be repeated other years. We also got a request for the school orchestra to give a recital in the church. This was agreed to and the Parish provided the tea.

That week we were delighted to have a visit from Gwyneth Tiarks, sadly now a widow. When Gwyneth saw a gentleman walk into the house and make for the kitchen, and then helping himself to the coffee on the table, she was a little worried as I was on the phone, so engaged the visitor in conversation. When I joined them, Gwyn said, "I'm afraid we don't know each other, but find we have a great many friends in common. There was laughter all round when I introduced the widow of Bishop John Tiarks to the retired Bishop Bulley formerly at Carlisle. We had told Cyril Bulley he might park his car on our drive, as long as he dropped in to coffee with us. He gave Raymond great support and help in Faringdon.

Faringdon Ups and Downs

Bernard Haines, an elderly solicitor, was a greatly respected Faringdon character. A church member whose wife had been the organist for many years until her death, he kept his office not unlike a Victorian solicitor's office, with files everywhere, many on the floor, yet Mr. Haines could at once reach for any file needed, and still had a very clear mind and memory. I asked him one day where he spent holidays. He said he did not take holidays, he was happier at work. Each day his housekeeper had his evening meal at the ready, as he always took the same bus home. When he did not turn up one evening she was worried, and after a while rang the police.

During the night the police arrived at the Vicarage to ask if Raymond could lead them to Mrs. Haines' grave, in case Mr. Haines had visited the grave and had a fall. Raymond took them into the vestry to look up the chart of graves, and they went off round the churchyard with torches, but found no Mr. Haines. Having asked the bus company if Mr. Haines had travelled on the usual bus, they

FROM LAND GIRL TO VICAR'S WIFE

said he had, but got off at a later stop outside the town. The next day the body of Mr. Haines was found in a deep ditch near the bus stop he had been taken to by mistake. There were signs of him having tried in vain to climb out of the ditch and having suffered a fatal heart attack. All Faringdon was shocked and saddened at the dreadful way poor Mr. Haines had died. The funeral drew a large congregation. There were those who hoped Mr. Haines' office would somehow be preserved as a bit of Faringdon history, but that did not come about.

We enjoyed great Fellowship with Father Cuthbert Smith, the Roman Catholic Priest, and saw more of him now that he had a church in Faringdon. Before he had a church and used a room in the corn exchange building for services, he sometimes came to the Vicarage to borrow a chalice, patten and wine and wafers if he had been delayed and hadn't time to return home. One morning he came to ask a favour – he wanted to lie flat on a floor, while waiting for a bus. He had a painful back ache. I thought quickly where he could lie down and not gather terrier white hairs on his black coat. I took him into Raymond's library where there was space for his tall figure.

I was busy in the kitchen and didn't hear Raymond come in, so he was very shocked to find Cuthbert flat out, and greatly relieved to find him alive and well. He drove him to his destination to save waiting for a bus. He had painful backache. I thought quickly where he could lie down and nor gather terrier white hairs on his black coat. I took him into Raymond's library where there was space for his tall figure.

From time to time, A.B. Williams and Marcelle had Marcelle's daughter and son-in-law, Jeremy Thorpe, and grandson Robert with them in church. They were well known in Faringdon, so when we heard on the news one day of the tragic death in a road accident of Jeremy's wife, most of the townsfolk were devastated. Raymond at once went down to the Old Barn in Great Coxwell, and found Marcelle at their fruit and vegetable stall, wearing dark glasses but carrying on with work as usual despite battling with the shock and grief of this great loss, and very concerned for Jeremy and Rupert.

Jeremy had just returned from electioneering in the south-west, and had returned to London by train while his wife wanted to pack. Marcelle said she had not only lost her daughter but also her best friend. They rang each other almost every day and she could not imagine life without her. She went off at once to join Jeremy for a few days, to give support to him and little Rupert.

Faringdon Church was given a very lovely white 'Festival' altar frontal in memory of her daughter, a valuable gift as all the church frontals were very worn. This gift inspired others to add more frontals, adding to the increasing improvements to the church. Visitors to All Saints felt the church compared favourably now with the famous Cirencester Church. Much credit for this was owed to the Flower Guilds' thought and skill and time given to lovely floral displays round the church.

Our very professional verger, Bert Hambridge was also dedicated to keeping the church very clean and tidy and spent much time clearing up after weddings the tiresome confetti on the church path. It was a sad day for All Saints when Bert felt he was running out of steam and must give up this work. Such dedicated professionals are rare in parish churches. A woman church cleaner was appointed to carry on. Happily, Bert did return soon after for Raymond to take his marriage. We all wished him joy but we all missed him.

In Christian Aid Week the clergy of the different denominations exchanged pulpits. The RC Priest was invited to preach in All Saints. Cuthbert Smith ended a very good sermon with the hope that all would return to the Catholic Church one day. Though Cuthbert expressed great joy in being in so old a pre-reformation church, and so beautiful a building, there were those not too pleased at having an RC priest in the pulpit, possibly the first since the Reformation. After the service Cuthbert invited Raymond and me to meet his Bishop of Portsmouth who was visiting him shortly. He was a delightful man and we had a long chat about the life of the church in general. When this Bishop became Bishop of Liverpool RC Cathedral and got on so well with the Anglican Bishop, David Shepherd, I was rather pleased to have met both these excellent priests. David, when

Captain of the English Cricket team had attended Bradford Cathedral and read one of the lessons, so I had met him as I left the Cathedral!

Maybe the Bishop was in Faringdon with Cuthbert arranging his retirement as we were sorry he retired soon after. We kept in touch by letter and hoped he was coming on a visit to us, but illness prevented him from coming. The very good looking Priest who succeeded Cuthbert, was brother of a film star of my young days, Anthony Bushell, whose films we rarely missed. Anthony was also a very handsome young man. I was told he had died young and that was the reason we saw no more of him in films.

About this time the easy relationship between our organist, Michael Perkins and Raymond, seemed to be fraying at the edges and there was tension between Peter Brown, our curate, and Michael. Possibly Peter's ministry was too evangelical for the rather High church Michael. At his work, Michael had worrying responsibilities and Raymond felt this was partly responsible for Michael's outbursts of temper at times, and for his impatience with church arrangements. Though Raymond tried to improve relationships with frequent talks it did not seem to ease the strained relationship. There began to be talk amongst the congregation about it being time for a change of organist but Raymond was reluctant to consider this as he hoped this was a passing phase. Michael was a very good organist and his choir gave very enjoyable recitals on Saturday evenings from time to time. A change of organist would undoubtedly cause a division in the church and good organists were not very easy to find.

1973 was a year of attending funerals of very dear friends and relatives, and was marked by the departure of Peter Brown and family; the PCC were not offering another curate. Peter was expected to stay for another year but the flat over a bank rented for them was now needed by the bank to house new Bank equipment, computers and the like. For Peter and Meg the expense of two moves within the year was not a happy thought. Though we were sad to see them go, there were parishioners who hoped this meant the end of the modernising of services. It was quite amusing to Raymond when he had a phone call from Peter's new Vicar a few weeks later to discuss some diocesan matter, and this Vicar then asked before ringing off, "By the way, was Peter Brown your curate?" Then, when told he was, this clergyman suggested there should perhaps be an association of Vicars that had Peter Brown as curate. We assumed the modernising of Vicars continued.

The Oxford Diocesan Conference in Swanwick made Peter's efforts to modernise us pale into insignificance. The form of services to which we were introduced appalled us. It seemed to be made up as we went along and in place of hymns we were given sentimental songs to Jesus and some happy-clappy songs. To take the sacrament we filed past the celebrants taking bread and wine as we passed. No reverent kneeling. When a young clergyman failed to find a seat he sat on the Holy Table during the sermon. Shattering though it was, we enjoyed an atmosphere of great Fellowship, and by the end of the week found we were very united and inspired by an outdoor Communion on the lawn, passing the Sacrament along the row. The lesson was about the feeding of the five thousand and somehow it came to life. We returned home with a lot to think about and found ourselves singing the sentimental songs to Jesus as we drove down the motorways back to Faringdon. Our services remained mostly based on the book of Common Prayer and with the well loved psalms and hymns, but we were helped to appreciate a new generation perhaps needed the new approach.

The year was one of sadness, starting with the sudden death of Little Coxwell Churchwarden, dear George Eyre-Brook, with a fatal heart attack. A retirement home was being built and his son was preparing to take over the farm. So very sad for his widow Diana. My mother who was living with us died in March. We three daughters were with her. Two months later my brother's wife Eileen Hall died very suddenly of a coronary. In July a cousin of Raymond's died. Having taken those funerals we were called back to Barrow for Raymond to take the funeral of our dear friend the Barrow organist, Margaret Taylor, to whom we owed so much, giving our daughters a very good start with their music and giving the church fifty years of a professional choir, adding so much to all the services.

Margaret's nephew told us Margaret had left her organ music to Elisabeth and I was to have her valuable Bosendorfer studio grand piano to pass on to one of the daughters one day. I had not returned from Barrow before hearing that Mrs. Birrell had died. She kept all the choir robes in order in St. Paul's and had made new surplices for Raymond while we were there. We couldn't stay to take her funeral as one of Faringdon deanery clergy, Vicar of Shrivenham, had died suddenly when just about to retire. The church was full for the required mass at his funeral.

In October one of Little Coxwell's great characters, Mrs. Rich, verger of the church, died at a great age. Having charge of the church and church key meant such a great deal to Mrs. Rich. The parish had a new key cut so that Mrs. Rich could keep her key and have it in her coffin with her. I lost a friend of many years when the Bournemouth Vicar who had prepared me for my confirmation died in October. We had corresponded from those early days and had visited him very shortly before he died. The suffragen Bishop of Carlisle, who often called on us in our Barrow days, died in November. We began to feel left behind.

Pressing on Regardless

1974 ran rather more smoothly and we were kept busy in between whiles, entertaining friends and family. Topsy and Towser provided entertainment with a litter of six lovely pups which found homes all too quickly. I was thankful that two found homes in Seaford when Topsy was restless looking for pups. As soon as she was taken to see them in local homes she settled down contentedly with Towser and there was no more fretting.

Faringdon problems made Raymond aware of his 61 years. Elisabeth was leaving Headington School for the Royal College of Music in Manchester to continue organ performance studies and Sara, now in the Sixth Form, was allowed to join the choir in St. Aldate's church and gained help with music studies from the organist there, as she hoped to study music at university. St. Aldate's Church a very alive evangelical church, strengthened her Faith too.

Norma Ingram, now locally known as a professional portrait painter, was engaged in much teaching, and pupils were very happy with their successes in local art exhibitions. Norma visited us most days and enjoyed morning coffee here with Bishop Bulley who looked in quite often. He was cheering company for Raymond who was feeling the need of a change and Bishop Bulley was always ready to help in church.

The new idea of getting laity to take parts of the service was for me very distracting. I thought often about St. Paul's days when Raymond, so well trained for the taking of services, took the services sometimes with lessons read by a church warden. Raymond took the intercessions from the centre of the aisle amongst the congregation and the atmosphere was of great togetherness and a feeling for all of a closenes to God. To me, shaking hands in the middle of a service, so unnecessarily interrupting one's communion with God, was a real trial. We did have coffee together after service to be sociable. I was quite evidently an 'old bottle skin', unable to take the new wine of modern worship.

In 1975 Michael Perkins was making it plain that he was not happy with evangelic visiting preachers and he and Raymond were no longer working in harmony. Raymond was not in good health, suffering with angina and had a nasty attack of shingles. The PCC made it plain to Raymond that there were many wishing for a change of organist. Raymond had tried to even things out with Michael, but this was never effective in getting a permanent return to a good relationship. Raymond asked for Michael's resignation as he did not want to be sacked, and Michael asked if he might continue until the summer and his girls had passed their school exams. This was arranged. Raymond had asked for a resignation from Michael in May, but this was not forthcoming. Michael told his choir he had been sacked. As Raymond had anticipated this matter divided the church.

There was an uncomfortable time with angry choir members

wishing for Raymond's resignation. After Michael left, taking most of the choir with him, we were glad to hear Michael was much happier taking a freelance choir to give concerts or helping in other churches.

All Saints was fortunate in getting the services of a very professional organist, who had run choirs in Canada. He was in England to take his FRCO and did some work for the BBC. Giles Bryant started at All Saints without choir, just as we were off on holiday to Cumbria, using our cousin's bungalow in Silecroft while they were holidaying in the south.

The Faringdon Church Choir rebuilt by Giles Bryant.

On attending Bowness Church, where we knew Canon Elliot as he had had Elisabeth and Sara in his choir while they were at St. Anne's School in Windermere; we met the Bishop of Carlisle as we were leaving the church. He asked Raymond if he liked the south. Raymond told him we were happier in the north and this the Bishop understood as he was happy in the north.

On our return to Faringdon we found Giles in good heart. He had visited homes in Faringdon and was encouraged by the response of children, mostly girls, willing to become choir members. He had no one yet apart from one choirman who had decided to remain in the choir. However, Giles at once roped in Elisabeth and Sara and said they would sing an anthem at Evensong, 'Lord for Thy tender mercies sake'. The choirman were to sing tenor, and Sara and Elisabeth soprano and alto and Giles bass. There were a few furtive looks back down the church when Raymond announced the anthem. We didn't have anthems, and no choir? The four voices carried perfectly through the church and as the congregation left many stopped to thank Giles and the Choir.

Soon Giles was training quite a big choir, and Raymond and Giles seemed to be on the same wavelength, often one coming to tell of a new idea to improve services just as the other was about to suggest it. Giles had a very good voice and sometimes sang the Litany or other parts of the service. When Giles told Raymond he would be leaving after a few months, we were disheartened. There were those criticising Giles by saying the organ was much too loud. Giles had filled in the gap so well and had got a good choir going. One bright boy had been taken into Salisbury Cathedral choir.

Meeting for prayer with Barbara, as usual, I complained to God about this new setback, but was cheered as I felt a great sense that all would be well. A few days later a letter from the Bishop of Carlisle arrived offering Raymond the livings of Lamplugh with Ennerdale and Kirkland in Cumbria near Cockermouth. I was soon happily packing in the attics, while Raymond spent much time in prayer. We set off to see Lamplugh and Ennerdale very soon after.

1976: *Faringdon Farewell in View*

● ●

When the invitaition from the Bishop of Carlise came, inviting us to inspect the parishes of Lamplugh with Ennerdale, we decide to travel to Elisabeth a day earlier and have a night with her in her Manchester flat, then set off early to Ennerdale the next day, 31st March. Sadly we got no glorious views, bogged down in wet thick mist all the way, and a cold journey. Finding no one at Ennerdale Vicarage, we found Tom Roper, a local farmer and Church warden, in St. Mary's. Ennerdale.

After a brief look at the little village church we were let into the Vicarage, higher up the hill, set surrounded by fields and with a view of the village below. I fell for the Vicarage at once, but it was painfully cold that day so we didn't dally too long but left Tom and went to look for the churchwarden in Kirkland, where the Mission Church was. Not finding the churchwarden there, we drove on to St. Michael's Lamplugh, the larger 'Mother church' of the combined parish. Tom Jaimeson was a very welcoming church warden and took a great pride in St. Michael's, founded by the Dickenson family. Ron Dickenson, the present member of the Manor house family, and Vicar's warden, joined us in the church. This one on a mountain top was even colder, but Raymond spent some time chatting with the Wardens about the parish while my teeth were chattering. Ron then took us over to Red How, the Manor House and, at last, the welcome offer of a wash and brush up – it was now after lpm and we'd been travelling since 7am!

Sitting by a wonderfully hot log fire, and having a glass of wine, we greatly enjoyed our half-hour or so with the Dickensons, and hearing all about the parish. We were expected by the Bishop in Carlisle within a short time so raced on, and were thankful to find a pub in Cockermouth still serving a basket of chips and hot coffee.

The Bishop seemed keen to have Raymond back in the Diocese though it was our first meeting with him. His secretary, who knew Raymond well, came in with a welcome cup of tea and cakes, so we set off back to Manchester well refreshed. We had plenty to discuss as we travelled, and the Bishop seemed to think the end of June would be a satisfactory time for our removal and that the parishes could be informed of the move some time in April. Raymond was to let the Bishop know as soon as possible if Raymond was quite happy to take on the three churches. I was hoping Raymond would be happy as I knew it was to be my sort of scene.

Though things had run smoothly since 1975, when the loss of Michael Perkins and the great upset for many had died down, we found life busier than ever. So many people took to dropping in to see us and many often ate meals with us, it was a happier year, though there were many parishioners who gave us all the cold shoulder at meetings or when meeting in the street. This was counterbalanced by a marked increase in congregations and great support from many who had previously kept in the background, yet had valued Raymond's ministry. Every single day that any of us were in the Vicarage we had visits from friends morning, noon and in the evenings, so we did little but entertain when not at meetings or parish visiting, or at services or hospital visiting and so on. It proved quite impossible to make a start on preparing for a move.

On 11th April, Raymond announced our departure was to be in June and our last Sunday would be 20th June. Sara's school days ended in June, and she had been accepted at Leeds University to study Music. Elisabeth had already started organ Performance studies at the Royal Northern College of Music in Manchester. All very convenient as we also were about to head North again.

Though Raymond's forthcoming departure cheered some, we were rather overwhelmed by a great increase of callers dropping in at all hours. As our days in Faringdon were running out, so the numbers increased. We took turns at disappearing into the kitchen to snatch a hasty lunch or tea, and in our last week were getting to work on the packing at 11pm and working into the early hours.

The parish put on a very happy farewell party in the Corn Exchange. Bishop Bulley had had tea with us and came to the party. The Bishop of Reading had been over to preach and spoke very kindly about Raymond's ministry; he seemed genuinely sorry we were leaving the Diocese. All very heartwarming. The churchwardens presented Raymond with a cheque for over £300, and I was given a most beautiful bouquet which I managed to preserve to travel North with us. That evening we realised what a great many really good friends we had made in our six and a half years in Faringdon, and many were intending to visit us in Ennerdale. A few were coming to Raymond's Induction at Lamplugh church on 1st July. On our last evening before leaving Faringdon, Raymond received a phone call from Michael Perkins, to wish him well in Ennerdale.

The Church Wardens and the Bell Ringers after the farewell afternoon of ringing many changes in appreciation of Raymond's ministry and support of the ringers.

Here We Go Again

••

The furniture removers were at the door at 7am. As they went back to drive the van in, neighbour Meriel Gillmore was amused to hear one say, "Crikey, could be James Mason himself."

Seeing the van at the Vicarage door, many parishioners on their way to the shops decided to come and have a final chat with us and wish us well – somewhat distracting while the removers were busy. We were pleasantly surprised to have Dr. Malcolm Warner and his wife call in to tell us that Malcolm was grandson of the Reverend Mortimer Warner, Raymond's Uncle and Godfather. As I went to the kitchen to get us coffee, the chairs I'd put out in the sitting room had been removed to the van so we sat on the floor to chat. We pointed out to Malcolm that the oil painting propped against the wall was of his great-grandmother, mother of Mortimer Warner. At this moment in came our artist friend Norma and, hearing she was a professional portrait painter, she readily agreed to paint a copy of this portrait for Malcolm. She took it off to return to us when we were next down South. Malcolm Warner and family bought Faringdon Vicarage shortly after as it was decided to build a smaller Vicarage for the next Vicar.

Elisabeth was delighted to return there to stay with the Warners when she had to play the organ for a service some time later. It was then Astley House, the original name when it had been the dower house of Faringdon House next door. The Warners had done a lot of work on the house and it was very lovely and not recognisable as our former home.

Until we finally left for the North at 3pm the callers continued and Cecil Blissett was last to see us off. He was sad Raymond was leaving. We were sad to say goodbye; Cecil and Nancy Blissett had been a wonderful support, always encouraging throughout Raymond's Ministry there and such good friends.

Faringdon and much of the south had been suffering a prolonged heatwave, causing drought, drying fields, lawns and gardens, so it was a refreshing sight to reach the lush green Cumbrian fields and fells. We felt we took the drought with us though, for almost as soon as we got to the north we had a prolonged heatwave, well into the autumn.

We staggered the journey to Ennerdale by leaving Sara and Topsy and Towser in Manchester and we had a night with our one time Barrow friend, Christine Lloyd, who now lived in Altrincham. We returned to Manchester early the next morning to collect the terriers, but Sara had to return to Headington School until Wednesday and Elisabeth was to join us in Ennerdale on Tuesday when her session ended. We got to Ennerdale to unload around 7pm, then had a night with cousins in Silecroft; they had offered to be with us the next day when the furniture was due to arrive in Ennerdale. We arrived in Ennerdale just after the removers had arrived. The unloading was achieved quite speedily, and we were grateful that cousins Alan and Betty stayed all day helping us to get beds made up and books unpacked in Raymond's study, and generally trying to turn the chaos into a home. They left us about 8pm and we were not too long getting to bed. The next morning before tackling more unpacking we decided to go to Whitehaven to do some shopping.

Whitehaven is an interesting port so we had a pleasant wander around before finding the good shopping area. We lunched in a café and after a good meal returned home to lay carpets. It was 1am before we finally finished work. Though a bit reluctant to make an early start we were soon unpacking again, but after an early lunch we did a quick shop in Whitehaven, and then I was busy getting bedrooms ready for Faringdon neighbours Meriel and her mother and son, Charles, and their Jack Russell 'Min', expected to arrive the next day, and we got more curtains up. In the afternoon we had our first visitors, the Rural Dean, Bill Kelly and his wife turned up to welcome us back to Cumbria and into his Deanery. Raymond and Bill Kelly knew each other well, both having worked in Barrow at the same time. They stayed to tea, and Raymond learned a bit about the Deanery.

We gave ourselves a bit of a break the next day, being Sunday, and went to St. Bees Priory to church, and enjoyed 8am. Communion and returned later to attend Matins and enjoyed a choral service with good choir and congregation. On attending Evensong we had a chat with the Vicar who was very welcoming. We got back to find Meriel, and mother, 'Midge', Charles and Min had arrived and had been let in by Tom Roper, in our absence. Though tired after a slow run held up by traffic jams, they were cheered by the lovely views and the situation of our new Vicarage.

Monday found us still getting curtains up, and a plumber came to install the washing machine. While Raymond was in Cockermouth, getting money from the bank, Lyn Oliver arrived, also from Faringdon, having booked a room at the local Inn, The Shepherd's Arms. Lyn had very poor sight so had her guide Labrador with her. Lyn spent the evening with us while Raymond was at a rehearsal in Lamplugh Church for the Induction to take place on Thursday 1st July. Raymond took Lyn to the Hotel when he returned and Meriel helped me to get more curtains up. The Vicarage had three living rooms and five bedrooms, so I was glad to be helped to finish with windows. We all got to bed about midnight.

While Raymond set off early to collect Elisabeth and two friends from the Northern College of Music, Manchester, Midge and I found life difficult with the plumber taking up much of the kitchen and hammering, making holes in the wall for washing machine pipes. Midge was trying to bake, Meriel was painting shelves and little Charles was fed up that no one had time to play with him. He cheered up when I set him to throw balls for Jet in the garden and Jet never tired of fetching balls. Raymond returned about 7pm. with Elisabeth, Julie and Robin. Soon we were all busy with tidying jobs, and Raymond and I got to bed at 1.15am.

Wednesday was the last of Sara's schooldays and she was quite happy to leave Headington and looked forward to life at Leeds Uni in the Autumn. Wednesday was intensely hot, but Raymond and I set off to collect Sara from Carlisle Station. We were not tempted to go round shops so spent a restful time in the cool of the Cathedral for a while and still had a long sit at the station, as Sara's train was an hour late. As Meriel and Charles and Elisabeth and friends went in search of somewhere to swim, Midge was thankful for some hours relaxing on her own.

Thursday, Induction day, was again very hot. Sara, Robyn, and Lyn did some grass cutting while I was busy getting beds ready for Cara, Jill and friend Flo and Aunt Grett, all coming to be with Raymond at his Induction, driving up from Bournemouth. Merry and Midge went shopping and were a help with catering for us all.

In the afternoon we had a visit from two of the girls' former teachers at St. Paul's Junior School, Barrow, Mrs. Matthews and Mrs. Railton, who had been favourite teachers of our two, and had enjoyed Raymond's years at St. Paul's.

There was a well packed church when we got to Lamplugh, but fortunately the church warden had pews reserved for us all.

ENNERDALE

The three places of worship in Lamplugh with Ennerdale.
Right: St. Michael's Lamplugh, Centre: St. Mary's Ennerdale Bridge;
Left: Kirkland Mission.

Our Delightful 'Swansong' Parish

• •

I always found the Induction service impressive and moving. I was full of memories of our previous parishes and the wonderful friends and joys each had brought. The warm greeting on arrival and the sadness of departure never really faded, and as we were pretty tired after the last farewells and the removal and now the new greetings I suddenly realised this must be our last parish as age was beginning to tell for us both. However, this time it was a feeling of coming home, because our days in the North had been so full of joy.

The service was joyful and there was a heartwarming welcome and sermon from the Bishop. The reception afterwards was staggering. Such a welcoming crowd, and a huge feast prepared for us all. It felt as if nearly all the clergy of the Diocese had travelled up to Lamplugh to welcome Raymond back, and we were made to feel we were well and truly amongst family. Our tiredness was forgotten in that joyful gathering and we were all pretty late getting away. It was a new experience for Aunt Grett, in her eighties; she thoroughly enjoyed the experience and I felt she had come in part to represent my Mother as she had lived with us in Barrow. Mrs. Matthew and Muriel Railton returned to the Vicarage with us to have a final coffee before returning to Barrow.

When Friday dawned, Meriel and Midge, Charles and Min set off to return to Faringdon to spread the news of our new Parish. Raymond, Elisabeth, Sara, Julie and Robyn decided on a visit to Silecroft to give the dogs and themselves a good walk along the sands, the dogs having had little attention since arriving back in the North, and we all had happy holiday memories of Silecroft. Cara drove Aunt Grett, Flo, Jill and me to Whitehaven, then to Cockermouth and Keswick. Again I found it too hot for comfort but the views were glorious as ever. It was Flo's 59th birthday so the girls gave her an informal concert of piano and violins.

We were allowed Saturday to continue settling in, especially as we still had guests to entertain. My sisters Cara and Jill decided to take Aunt Grett to Silecroft to see Alan and Betty; from there they went on to Muncaster Castle, and then to see Ennerdale Water and the lovely surrounding mountains. Lyn did some grass cutting, and was then invited to do some bellringing. Julie was leaving us so we took her with Elisabeth and Robin to Kendal to see her on to her train. Having taken Elisabeth and Robyn home for them to exercise the dogs, Raymond and I rushed on to Heversham and were five minutes late getting to John Hancock's Induction, thereafter as Vicar of Coniston. We had a few minutes talk with John and Margaret before returning home, and after all that we were home and had had tea before Cara returned with Aunt Grett, Flo and Jill who had enjoyed their day out and about.

Farmer Tom Roper, Vicar's Warden,with Raymond at St. Mary's Church, Ennerdale.

Raymond wanted a chat with Mr. Roper about the Ennerdale services and I went along and we had a long session with him, and were very happy with all he told us. He gave Raymond a list of church members who would appreciate an early visit, and as he spoke of each he added, "You will like them, they are very nice people." From the few we had already met this came as no surprise. We soon learnt that the family feeling about Ennerdale, Lamplugh and Kirkland was because so many of the local people were quite closely related.

143

Sunday services were a bit exhausting, starting with Communion at Ennerdale, and leaving while the last hymn was sung to rush to Kirkland for their Morning Prayer service, then on to take Communion in Lamplugh Church. We reckoned the attendance at the three churches was about eighty parishioners and that was considered a little more than usual to meet the new Vicar. I was soon to realise that my idea of a restful retirement parish was not working as I'd imagined. It soon became obvious that three parishes, with widely scattered homes, was going to have Raymond always on the go, visiting and taking services at the three churches, not just on Sundays, but with mid-week services and of course weddings, baptisms and funerals. Raymond also fitted in services in other churches at times.

I was soon as busy as ever preparing for one lot of visitors after another, while Raymond was trying to get out and about to get to know church members and those needing regular visits at home. For a start Raymond was driving some of the visitors who came for the Induction to Kendal or to Barrow stations to see them off. The family left to return to work before Cara and Jill were off on holiday to Switzerland. Elisabeth and Sara and a school friend, Rhiannon, had been invited to go with Cara and Jill on this holiday, so in between visiting some of the church members with us, they were busy planning how to pack for this two weeks away.

Elisabeth had visited the churches and tried out the chamber organ in Lamplugh and found it in need of an overhaul. Some of the notes would not play. Though Kirkland chamber organ was reasonable it needed someone to pump it. As for poor Ennerdale there was an ancient harmonium type organ and the electric blower made almost more noise than the organ. This instrument was past having much done to it. The organist was a delightful elderly lady, Miss Ireland who did very well on such a worn out instrument. It was rather sad that so good a musician should have so poor an instrument but she was resigned to it.

Meeting with Marjorie and Tom Jaimeson, churchwarden at their bungalow, within sight of Lamplugh Church, was a delight. We were given a warm welcome, were made to stay for some tea, and told a lot about the church and members. The church was clearly their life. They took great pride in looking after it and keeping it in good order. They were both very devout and hard working. Marjorie had been in domestic service and she referred often to 'when I served my time.' Sara hearing this one day asked me as we left, "Was Mrs. Jaimeson in gaol?" There could be no one less likely to serve her time in gaol unless out to convert prisoners!

It was suggested we should call on elderly Mrs. Abraham living nearby, a very regular attender at Lamplugh Church. We had met Mrs. Abraham at the Induction. Her ancestors had connections with Quakers who I think were connected with the founders of the Society of Friends near Ulverston. It was an interesting visit. She told us her daughter, who was approaching forty was shortly to get married to a hospital colleague, that she would like Raymond to take the service and I would be getting an invitation. Raymond was advised by the Jaimesons of a house he need not visit as the folk were Roman Catholics. We did however call on them, having had their home pointed out to us, and they seemed very pleased to meet the new Anglican Vicar, and conversation flowed easily.

There was enough domestic work for me to let Raymond do much visiting on his own as we were not yet unpacked, and I had to get bedrooms ready for the next visitor invasions. Having a very roomy Vicarage we were getting lots of letters from folk wanting to see our new surroundings and parishes.

As I walked the dogs I got into conversation with passers- by as they all knew who I was. This led to invitations into farmhouses where I at once felt very much at home as I had worked on farms in the Land Army.

Settling to Work

Mrs. Atkinson's son Cyril was churchwarden at Kirkland. Both Cyril and his mother gave much time to caring for the church. It was used as a hall for in the week and Mrs. Atkinson did a wonderful job keeping it clean and tidy for the Sunday services. Considering she had reached her eighties we were worried she was overdoing the work, and one lady said, "That church will be the death of you."

To which Mrs. Atkinson said, "What happier place to die than in serving God in His Church."

She had the same devotion to her church as the Jamiesons had to Lamplugh, and the Ennerdale Church members had to their church. This did not make it too easy to suggest that the three services each Sunday morning should be changed and perhaps one could have Evensong while two had the Morning Communion. At the first PCC representing all churches Raymond put forward this proposal, explaining he was rather sad he could not see the congregations out of church, and have a chat with them, as time just didn't allow it. To his joy they all liked the idea realising it was quite a strain to take the three services one after the other and explained that had been arranged during the interregnum, as it suited the visiting clergy.

Lamplugh and Ennerdale liked the idea of having a Matins in place of Communion one Sunday in the month. I was glad of this as I was taking Communion at all three churches because it seemed a lack of Fellowship not to take communion with some of our church members. Towards the end of July, Ennerdale suddenly had a full church when sixty Scouts, who were at an Ennerdale camp. All came to the morning service. Considering many were quite young and on an exciting holiday, they all seemed to listen intently to the sermon. Their presence added much to the service and they sang well.

Setting to work was frequently interrupted for a start by a constant stream of visitors from near and far wanting to see our new home and surroundings. One of the first was a former Barrow parishioner, Miss Spedding, brought by her niece. We had visited Miss Spedding's home a lot in the past as her mother lived with her until she was over 104 years-old. Miss Spedding in her seventies, looked after her. Raymond and I had paid a visit to the Speddings on the hundredth birthday of Mrs. Spedding and she was just off to greet people at a local hotel where they were to celebrate. When she was 103 Raymond took her to a shop in Tonbridge to buy a new hat. The assistant ran to get her a chair. "I came for a hat, not a chair," said Mrs. Spedding. Raymond visited her the night she died. It was late on a wintry night. Mrs. Spedding chided the Vicar for turning out on so wretched a night and told her daughter to give the Vicar a brandy. Raymond did not accept a brandy but talked with Mrs. Spedding and left after praying with her; she died very soon afterwards. Her daughter said her mother clearly saw relatives in Heaven coming to greet her as she was talking to them by name and holding out her arms to hug them. Miss Spedding felt left out as she saw no one, but was so happy for her mother. The church put their flag at half-mast on the day of her funeral Mr. Bundy, headmaster of St. Paul's School asked at assembly if anyone knew why the flag flew at half-mast.

"Yes sir," piped up a little lad, "The Vicar's dog has been shot." (Buzz, one of our young Jack Russells, had been shot by a simple-minded lad who was moving sheep, though the dog was nowhere near the sheep, and this sad story was reported in the press.)

Miss Spedding had not heard of this and was amused to hear the Speddings had a light lunch and tea with us, and then I was busy preparing bedrooms to accommodate our Faringdon Secretary of the PCC Peggy Spinage. Raymond's brother was coming the same day for a two-week holiday. A choir member from Faringdon, Colin Bessant and family, were to be caravanning in Ennerdale also. A holiday they had planned before knowing we were to move there, so they hoped to use our bathroom for occasional baths. Peggy was surprised to be greeted by the Bessants when she arrived. Bernard had planned to get some work done in the garden when Raymond was busy. While getting ahead with a bit of catering and cooking, we had a phone call from Dr. Christopher Tiarks, to let us know his Mother had just died of a distressingly painful cancer.

I had lived on and off with the Tiarks in Bradford and had been married from their Vicarage, so this was very sad news. Raymond was asked if he could take the funeral in Birmingham, as the Archbishop of Canterbury (formerly Bishop of Bradford) was to be in hospital for a minor treatment on the day of the funeral. This was arranged and we remembered that, only a year or two before, Gwyneth had said that when we next visited she would take us to see John's grave. We little thought it would be Gwyneth's funeral that would lead us there, but there was consolation that she was now free of pain and hopefully now rejoining John.

At the funeral while Raymond was taking leave of mourners at the grave Douglas Webster, Canon of St. Paul's Cathedral (whom we often met in Bradford Vicarage, as a great friend of the Tiarks) handed me a copy of the Church Times telling me to read the obituary sent by the Archbishop about Gwyneth. It read almost word for word what Raymond had said in his address at the funeral service. Douglas was very impressed with Raymond's taking of the service and his address, having never before heard Raymond preach. When Douglas visited us it was of course always Douglas who came to preach.

Having spent the evening with Ann Tiarks, Remfrey and husband and Julian chatting over old times and catching up on news of their family, we retired early as we planned to leave before 6am the next morning to return to Ennerdale before the traffic built up.

On arriving home I found I was to miss attending the Ennerdale Annual Agricultural Show, as a carpet firm had decided to come that day to lay the new carpets we had been awaiting for some weeks. This was a real disappointment, but Raymond and the girls spent the day there, and I felt very frustrated at having to wait a whole year before enjoying this event. However, Raymond, Elisabeth and Sara made use of the day getting to know a lot of the locals.

We were ready for a holiday in August and went to Bournemouth to stay with family, but managed to stay a night at Bishop Bulley's home on the way down. The Bishop made us very welcome and it was a chance to exchange news. Bishop Bulley was pleased that a Cumbrian Vicar known to him, Jack Whittaker, had accepted the living of Faringdon, and looked forward to being able to help him. On our return to Ennerdale it was sad to see Elisabeth and Sara off back to College and I missed their help in the home. However, Evelyn Campbell, retired teacher who had been a family friend since my very early days, came to stay. Evelyn was thrilled with such a wonderful setting for our Vicarage, and said she felt it was a taste of Paradise. We had happy phone calls from both Sara and Elisabeth very content with their teacher training courses. Evelyn said she would send her academic gown to Sara in case it was needed for school events one day.

Friend of my childhood days, Evelyn Campbell, comes to stay and considers Ennerdale 'Paradise'.

The Vicarage.

Autumn 1976

• •

Living among these impressive Cumbrian mountains and fells the beauty of the autumn colours was breathtaking. Even if a good artist were able to capture the astonishingly red bracken clothing the hills, and capture all the golds and varied greens and browns against clouds and blue skies, I think it would be considered the poetic licence of the artist. It was certainly very uplifting while walking the dogs up the fell opposite the Vicarage to an ancient stone circle. I liked to rest there and look across to the sea near Whitehaven in the distance.

The farm just across the road from the Vicarage, 'Fell End', was owned by John and Mary Mitchell, who very quickly became great friends, and I was given permission to wander with my dogs in their field as often as I liked. John was not only a busy and successful farmer, but he and his wife both put in time working at Windscale nuclear power station not far away. My sheep dog Jet kept control of my Jack Russells when off the lead in John's fields. If they attempted to go through a hedge where sheep might be grazing, Jet would quite roughly shepherd them back to me. In fact so roughly that they used to scoot back to me as soon as I gave Jet the command to bring them back. In those fields were buzzards and ravens and, in lambing time (if John and Mary were out), I used Jet to chase them off, or they could attack lambs while they were being born. Herons and sometimes kingfishers fished in a stream by the fields. One day John told me they had just disturbed a pine martin while working amongst pine trees – a rare sight so they were cheered to know there were still some around.

John and Mary went through a rough time when they were accused of sheep stealing by an unfriendly local. This led to John and Mary going to Carlisle Crown Court for days on end. John was proved not guilty, as the locals had been sure was the case, as John had many friends who had known him since he was young and knew him to be an honest and hard-working farmer.

One day when walking the dogs to Ennerdale Water, I met with a lady trying to help a heifer bogged down in a ditch. Her husband was unable to help as he had a leg in plaster up to his thigh. I tied up the dogs up and waded in, trying to help the heifer on to her side near the bank so that her legs were freed and we could perhaps roll her on to the bank. She struggled and tried to co-operate, but it was an effort, but eventually she was lying on the bank exhausted. Jim and Hilda then introduced themselves and enquired where I lived. They were a bit shaken to learn I was the wife of the new Vicar. They were quite relieved to find I had had experience of handling cattle. Jim said he would stay with the heifer who was soon due to calve, and let her rest till ready to get up and have a quiet walk to the farm.

That was the start of a good friendship as we often called into their farm where their animals were their pets. Lovely sheep dogs, cats and hens at home in the kitchen. Geese and ducks about and cattle in a nearby field. They had two daughters, one married and hoping shortly to present them with their first grandchild.

When a grandson was born we called in at the farm and they were very excited to have a grandson, but had not yet seen him. Alas, soon after, we were told, the baby boy had spina bifida and could not survive long. We felt so sad for them and it brought back to us the heartbreak we suffered when our first born died in the womb. We were never more sad than at the funeral that followed so soon after, seeing Grandad walking up the church aisle carrying his grandson in a little white coffin. There were few with dry eyes as we left the church. Happily, in time their son in law and daughter were able to console all with two lovely little daughters full of good health. Attending the baptisms gave great joy.

Encouragements

Down towards the lake lived Mr. and Mrs. Hill with their teenage daughter Susan. Though Mr. and Mrs. Hill were not regular attenders Susan was often in church, and offered to try to start a Sunday School for little children. She came to the Vicarage to take part in Bible studies and get help preparing lessons. She found someone to help in Anne Harrington, a school friend. Sadly there was no rush of children, but one did turn up. There was a rush for children to attend Confirmation classes and seventeen enrolled. As most were not churchgoers, but sent along by parents, there was great dismay to learn part of the preparation was regular attendance at church, so some signed off after the first session. Those that stayed the course used to come to the Vicarage for a cup of tea and cake before class, having come straight from school. Susan got some of these interested in the idea of a Youth Fellowship after Evensong on Sundays, and this went well.

When Susan and friends decided they would like to join the church choir in Ennerdale Miss Ireland, who battled with the old harmonium was delighted and had choir practice sessions with the girls in the Vicarage. This was not welcomed by the farmer's wives who had formed the choir for some years, but they realised it was encouraging church attendance among the youngsters so accepted the idea, but some of the wives were less often seen in church.

That old harmonium horrified Elisabeth when she was home, knowing it must be agonizing to Raymond in particular, since he was brought up to very good church music. Elisabeth talked to an organ builder who was teaching organ building at their college. One day, quite out of the blue, Mr. Sixsmith, organ builder, dropped in to call on us. He said he was interested to see the harmonium in the church that he was told about by Elisabeth. Raymond brought Mr. Sixsmith back to the Vicarage for lunch with us as we had kept him for some time. He was sure he could make a small suitable pipe organ to be quite adequate for Ennerdale, and a great improvement on the harmonium which had a blower attached that tended to make more noise that the poor harmonium. It would be at an economical price, as organs go, because some churches were changing to electronic machines and there were quite good second-hand organ pipes available reasonably. The price he quoted was so reasonable the PCC at once started an appeal for funds. It met with a great response. When I told Mary and John Mitchell how we hoped to get this organ, John went to his desk, scooped up loose notes under the lid and handed me ten £10 notes and said they would be glad to respond to that appeal as a thank you for the Vicar's support and prayers during their tiresome court case.

When the cost was raised, Mr. Sixsmith and a colleague had the organ built and in place and ready for action all in a day. I said to the colleague, I supposed we should insure the organ, and he agreed that would be wise but said the insurance must be for a lot more than we were paying for the organ as Mr. Sixsmith had only charged for the materials and nothing for the work done. Elisabeth was asked to play a little recital to show what a versatile little organ it was. After this recital a gentleman at the back confessed to having taped the recital without asking permission as he had arrived late, and asked if he would let her know of future recitals at any Cumbrian church, so I was given one or two tapes of her recitals by this gentleman.

Elisabeth gives a recital on the new organ, Ennerdale.

Farmer Jim Hinde living in the village was people's warden at Ennerdale Church, and gave a lot of time to keeping the churchyard tidy and was often on sidesman duties. His wife Mary was a member of the choir. Mary introduced me to the Mother's Union and the Women's Institute. This was a help in getting to know the villagers and the meetings were very enjoyable.

A lady turned up in her car one day and introduced herself and her husband as Dorothy and Stanley Hocking, whose home was in Edinburgh, but having a cottage in Lamplugh with the delightful name of 'Witts End', they often spent time in Lamplugh and Ennerdale. They had a clergyman son who came sometimes with his family. Dorothy often visited the Vicarage and was a keen church member, so they quickly became good friends. We frequently received invitations to tea with them and their daughter Ella, who was a social worker.

It was very sad when Dorothy, doing one of her many good deeds, helping a young man to push his car up the hill outside their cottage, had a stroke the next day. Though making a good recovery she gave up driving, so we didn't see so much of the Hockings. Not long after Stanley died, and Dorothy died soon after. We were all sad to hear, not long after, that Ella also had died. John Hocking kept in touch for years after but we didn't meet again. They were all greatly missed in Cumbria.

Sitting in Kirkland Church one morning near to Mrs. Atkinson in the back pew, I was worried that she was fidgeting and restless and eventually I asked quietly what was wrong. Very quietly she whispered that she had put on an old skirt over her Sunday outfit while working at home and had forgotten to take it off. Hence all the wriggling and fidgeting. We sat stuffing handkerchiefs in our mouths trying to silence uncontrollable giggles while she eventually managed to drop it off and roll it under her seat. I did love Mrs. Atkinson. She had a lovely sense of humour.

Off-Comers Settle in Ennerdale
• •

Much of the Lake District being a National Park, it seemed sad that many farmers were not given permission to have a cottage built on their farmland for retirement, yet, lo and behold, a row of very town like dwellings appeared in the village. There was talk of more houses to be built in a field across a stream opposite the new houses. This building was delayed as the builders were told they would have to build a new safe bridge over the stream as the footbridge would not take the traffic. This bit of Ennerdale was outside the National Park restrictions, hence the arrival of a row of houses which were very quickly sold and filled with young couples with children. Though the row of houses looked out of place to many, they were pleased to have more school pupils and new life in the village.

Raymond and I visited all these friendly young people and, though not uninterested in church life, said their husbands mostly worked away and were only home at the weekends, so that kept them at home to keep the family together while Dad was with them.

I got to know most of these young wives. Lyn and Ken Hill had three young daughters – Deborah, Ailsa and Sarah. Lyn wanted to get the girls attending church, so in holidays I suggested they came to the 10am Communion services on a Wednesday morning. Only one lady attended regularly, Mrs. Slack, and she would not mind the young children coming for that service, even if they should be restless. Lyn's neighbour, Sue Hoyle, had three youngsters – James and twins Emma and Joanne; Maureen Valkes and Charles had daughter Donna and, soon after their arrival in Ennerdale, added twin girls, Gina and Dawn, to their family. Jacqui Newcombe lived in Lamplugh but liked the idea of attending Ennerdale on Wednesday with her young son Andrew.

These Mums and their seven little ones made a nice congregation at the Wednesday services and I persuaded the Mums to let the babes wander at will round the church during the service, as we kept the door shut and to keep little ones sitting through a service which they wouldn't understand and of which they could soon tire.

Young James House, who had loved to escort Raymond from the sanctuary to the vestry, and ply him with questions, joined a church choir when they had moved from Ennerdale. I was delighted to receive a lovely photo of the Hill daughters, all grown up and the older two bridesmaids at the marriage of young sister Sarah. We grew very fond of those families and they all gave help in parish affairs.

Ennerdale Vicarage. In the centre Maureen and first set of twins.

I greatly enjoyed the Women's Institute meetings when I was free to attend and often took along guests staying with us. At the meetings we sat round in a ring which made the meeting less formal than sitting in rows. The President was given a top table for refreshment time, and the rest of took our own snacks and enjoyed time for a chat. The Mother's Unions would have good parties from time to time, and sometimes put on a wonderful concert by the members. There was a great family feel throughout all the organisations of the three churches.

News from the three parishes was often conveyed to us by our postman. Harry Wylie dropped in for a tea or coffee most mornings. He was everyone's friend, and if anyone was ill Harry would often do shopping for them while on his round. He sometimes had a very treacherous journey in his van in severe wintry weather, even finding himself snowbound sometimes. Harry was often one of the first to hear of youngsters getting engaged, or babies having arrived and of sudden deaths or illness that called for a Vicar's visit. When working near the school the kiddies would all be singing out to him, "Postman Pat, Postman Pat, where's your black and white cat?"

When Harry was on duty he used to come straight into the kitchen, and could pour himself a coffee if we were on the phone or in the garden, as I had the essentials ready on the table for droppers in.

When Sara was on holiday John Mitchell would call to see if Sara would help him round up sheep on the fell. It was her job to run up the fell ahead of John to open gates. John sometimes called around 6am to ask if Sara was up. She soon was, as soon as she heard John's voice and would appear in shabby old jeans and pullover ready for the fray. She had lessons in sheep shearing, but left John to tidy their heads and faces. On a morning when John wanted help to get sheep loaded for market, Sara disappeared and didn't return till evening, having had supper with John and Mary. After helping to get lambs into the market ring an elderly farmer came over to ask, "What did your lambs fetch then lassie?"

John was at hand to tell him. Not content with just doing the occasional day with John and Mary, Sara offered to help at the Shepherds Arms Hotel. Her offer was accepted and she was paid for general domestic work, cleaning bedrooms, remaking beds, polishing the loo seats and also helping a bit in the bar.

The daughters had little experience of domestic work in our Vicarages, but Sara got a very good training at the hotel and got on well with Mr. and Mrs. Bott, whose sister Jacqui came with her boy to the Wednesday Service and coffee gathering. Sara also had a lesson in spinning sheep's wool from Mrs. Bott senior who lived in a cottage near the hotel. Both daughters enjoyed country life.

Elisabeth joined Sara when John was busy with the harvest, and they found it quite tough work stacking hay bales on to a trailer. It was a refreshing break for them from college studies and they got to know the church people well, though away so much, as Elisabeth was often at an organ, and Sara very competent at the piano when the need arose.

During 1977 Bishop Richard Hare who had been our Archdeacon in Barrow days, put us in touch with a former Bradford ordinand, now a Clergyman, with whom he had lost touch some years earlier. This friend, Laurence Hoyle and his wife Margaret, were now in charge of a conference centre, Lamplugh House, in East Yorkshire. The Bishop had told Laurie that Raymond was now in a parish called Lamplugh so Laurie at once got in touch and invited us to spend a weekend with them and to join in a Renewal conference. We were intrigued by the number of church denominations that were represented. This was an opportunity to experience the Charismatic Renewal now springing up worldwide in churches, though this movement was causing great division in some churches where there was an effort to organise this revival.

In Lamplugh House we experienced deep Christian Fellowship brought about with much Faith and prayer. There was frank discussion and sharing of worries and problems. Raymond felt he was experiencing the true Fellowship he had enjoyed in Wycliffe Hall when in training for the Ministry. There was praying in tongues and interpretations and singing in the Spirit, refreshing and strengthening us in the Faith. A clergy wife asked if she could discuss her marriage problem with me, and I suggested she would be better helped by Bishop Hare. I was pleased to see her go off with the Bishop; some time later she came to tell me that she and her husband had been so helped by Bishop Hare, they were happier now than for some years. Such was the joy for many attending this conference and we returned home greatly refreshed and encouraged.

Many felt a new closeness to God through having the laying on of hands and felt very conscious of the indwelling Holy Spirit and were used to bring healing to others. We were grateful to Laurence and Margaret for the real uplift of the weekend with them.

Wintry start, 1979

• •

I have never felt much of a thrill when snow falls. Even as a child I was not too eager to get freezing hands throwing or receiving snowballs. Snow in Cumbria made life hard for shepherds and sheep and for cattle, and made hard work of feeding stock. The mountains did look magnificent in gleaming white clothing, but I felt sad for the hungry creatures and birds, and wished fields still had the trees or sheds for shelters. The stone walls offered some protection and, built very skilfully with loose stones, sheep buried near the walls were often able to survive burial in the snow by getting some air through the loose stones. John Mitchell still kept his hedges in very good order, skilfully making them a real shelter by weaving the branches in the traditional way, and so filling gaps.

There was a Sunday when we could not get to Kirkland and Lamplugh churches as the roads were blocked by deep snow drifts. Overnight the roads became very icy and treacherous. One morning I was not sure we were going to get out of the Vicarage, but up rolled John on his tractor to clear snow from our garage and doors. There was no shortage of help for anyone in need and our good postman Harry was at the grocers buying food for lots of people on his round, though he had difficulty in getting the van to the homes on the icy roads.

In March, when the weather was a worry, dear Sara rang up from Leeds to say she was bringing quite a crowd of friends to us, to help her celebrate her 21st birthday, and that Elisabeth was travelling up by train to Carlisle in the hope Dad could meet her there in the car. I tried in vain to persuade them to postpone the gathering until the roads might be safer.

Sara assured me she was coming with a girl who was a good driver and had asked the AA about the route. She couldn't stay to talk as the three were in the car waiting for her. I persuaded Raymond to get to bed and I would wait up for them. They were setting off in the dark and I was sure we were in for a long wait to see them arrive if they managed to get through. I was not greatly cheered when I got a phone call from Sara to tell me they were well on the way but she was in a phone box while police were pushing the car up an iced road. It was about 11.30pm. when I saw headlights at the top of the twisty hill from Kirkland down into Ennerdale, and I prayed I should not see the lights suddenly pointing at the sky. It was narrow and had a deep drop one side of the road, so my relief was great when I saw them arriving down our long drive. The driver admitted she would not want to do that drive again, but they were all very cheerful and glad to have achieved the drive. The second car arrived soon after.

Raymond and I had managed to get Elisabeth safely home from Carlisle station in the afternoon, but the drive up a long hill after Cockermouth was alarming; there were several damaged or overturned cars parked on grass verges along our route. Raymond dealt with the iced roads very confidently, though we did skid about from side to side a bit on the way, but were safely on our side. It was wonderful to see all safely in and in very high spirits after the drive.

There was much fun and games going on the next day and rehearsing by some to give a concert to Sara. One young man had composed a violin musical tribute to Sara for this occasion, which delighted her but she felt it a bit beyond her to play. It was some time before the visitors retired to bed, and from our room we heard much rushing about and merriment. It seems Sara's room curtains fell down when she tried to pull them, the bed legs gave way when she sat down, and many uncomfortable items were in her bed.

Elisabeth and the other girls suffered objects in the bed but Sara's room got most attention. The next morning Raymond and I were first up, and there was still a fair bit of running around, much laughter and banging on doors. Eventually I went up to find that the lads' punishment for the evening activities was to find themselves locked in their bedroom early morning. Eventually all were up and after breakfast set off to be taken for a good walk round Ennerdale Water.

Mrs. Jaimeson had made a lovely cake for Sara, so the Jaimesons and the Dickensons came to tea to meet these students. Tom Roper came across too and they were treated to some music by the students.

The weekend passed happily; snow and ice had given way to sunshine and a thaw, so I felt happier about their return journeys. The Vicarage was incredibly quiet as I changed bedding and had a tidy up.

Elisabeth seemed to spend much time with a fellow student, Gordon Stewart, a very talented organist, and she was useful to him as he gave many concerts and Elisabeth often went with him to turn pages for him. They were such good pals and Gordon a delightful character with a great sense of humour, and we enjoyed many visits to Gordon who put us up at his house when we visited Elisabeth in Manchester. I wondered at times whether we were to have a Scotsman as son-in-law, but Elisabeth assured me Gordon's only love was the organ.

Though I was hoping in April we would have warmer weather for Easter as I had visitors lined up to come again, Sara was enjoying skiing in Scotland with student friends. However we were cheered that the cost of the organ in Ennerdale had now been met. Though congregations had thinned a bit during severe weather they were building up again; holidaymakers and camping guides and Scouts added to our numbers some weeks. Maundy Thursday brought in a more encouraging congregation for the evening Communion commemorating the Last Supper. At the service a year ago only Queenie Slack had joined the Fountain family for the service, but we were eleven this time. Holidaymakers Mrs. Ayling and two daughters, Ken and Lyn Hill who were pretty regular attenders, Nurse Mabel Proctor and Mrs. Atkinson from Kirkland joined Sara and me. It was a quiet and impressive service. I was feeling sad for the shepherds, having been very grieved on my walks to keep coming across dead or dying lambs. John had a fair few in their home, rescued after birth, having been deserted by their mums, who had no milk for them after a cruel winter. I was shocked to have seen big lorries filled with dead lambs coming away from some farms. My prayers were with the farmers who had had a wretched winter. Some of our friends came to join us for an evening prayer group. Sara stayed in the village to 'baby sit' at the Shepherd's Arms.

Sara comforting a deserted lamb.

On Good Friday there were morning services at Kirkland and Lamplugh and at Ennerdale an Evening meditation in an attentive atmosphere which was very helpful. Sara played the organ for the hymns. On Saturday the family were assembled. Liz had arrived the evening before and Cara and Jill had arrived in time for Easter Sunday and were to stay until Friday; Elisabeth also was to return to College on Friday and Sara back to Leeds on Saturday. The Easter services were so well attended by 138; we wished the church could be as full every week.

John and Mary Mitchell were busy trying to get deserted lambs accepted by 'foster Mum' sheep, and rescuing the new born, so missed the morning services. Raymond took an evening service of Communion just for the Mitchells, so the family decided to join them at that. Sara had been at the farm and had successfully delivered a lamb for a ewe in difficulty.

The Spring brought more snow and even in May we were still getting snow showers, though the sunny spells soon cleared the showers. We had a succession of visitors coming for holiday and I seemed to spend my time between meetings and services and entertaining in the Vicarage, always preparing meals or baking cakes or biscuits. Raymond's angina was somewhat troublesome, and I was put on to stronger tablets to control blood pressure. Though always busy we enjoyed the activities and felt very much at home in Ennerdale with so many wonderfully kind friends.

We had a fairly anxious sounding Sara on the phone from time to time as she worked hard for her degree exam. On 18th June she rang up to tell us she had achieved a BA Hons. 2.2 pass degree in Music. She proposed to go on to a teacher training college. At the same time, Elisabeth finished a postgraduate year at the Royal Northern College in Manchester and was also going on to a teacher training college.

As something of a celebration, my sisters decided to take us all four to Switzerland for a week at the end of June. This kind and generous idea couldn't have come at a more welcome time as we were both pretty tired. We had recently met church people who related to us what a wonderful church they had been attending. It was very lively and well attended and such an excellent Vicar with great ideas, and doing so much for the young people.

I had a feeling this was meant to suggest Raymond should be doing much more in the parish. I could have been wrong but I said this church sounded very like our Barrow church, where the Vicar was youngish and had two young enthusiastic curates to help get in the youngsters. Visiting is so much easier in a town as the houses are much closer together and so less time spent on travelling, and on the whole people have more time for out of work activities.

Yes, our friend agreed there were two curates and the Vicar was quite young, and it was a city parish. A very different scene from Ennerdale and Lamplugh, and one elderly Vicar with three churches. However, this remark did get us thinking that maybe it was time we made some decision about retirement. Though clergy are expected to retire at seventy years, not all have the good health to stay on that long. While on holiday we did think about it a lot. Raymond did not want to retire, but felt it might be kind to the parish to make way for a fitter clergyman, and possibly a younger one. Raymond came to no decision but felt God would advise when it was time to give up.

The journey home from Interlaken took us through France in the train on 14th July, Raymond's birthday, and all the flags were out – France was celebrating the Bastille Day. Raymond and I spent a night at Gordon's home in Manchester on our way back to Ennerdale, and felt refreshed after the lovely week.

Summer 1979

• •

June weather at last turned to summer and we got more attending the Wednesday Communion. The children had mostly tired of running around during the service and little Sara Hill would sit in front of the pews telling stories to her doll, which I enjoyed. The rest would bring toys or books and sit with Mum. Grannies started to come to this service also and my coffee group grew. The dining room became quite a nursery as the Mums brought a great collection of toys and were able to enjoy coffee and adult chat without too much interruption. When I had visitors they would often join us in the front garden having open-air coffee and enjoying the mountain views. They were happy occasions and lovely to watch the children developing so quickly, especially the two sets of twins. We also often had a coffee evening to raise funds. Many put a lot of work into sale goods but we rarely raised more than £40 in an evening, every bit helped towards the Summer Fête.

July 19th was a great day in Leeds. Cousins Bill and Mary, who lived in Leeds and had entertained Sara to many meals and outings while she was at the University, gave us lunch with Sara before we set off to see Sara receive her Degree. Sadly, the Duchess of Kent, who had presented Elisabeth with her organ performance degree, was unwell and unable to present the Music degrees in Leeds as had been planned, but we enjoyed the day and seeing Sara posing for her photo holding her degree certificate. It was good to have seen both girls successful in their exams.

Our next job was to entertain a Church Army captain with a mini mission in the villages. Dennis Oxley, Helen and Jonathan turned up and had lunch with us; Tom Roper came to welcome them and to find out how best we could help. After lunch they went to a reception meeting in Kirkland. On Sunday the services at all three churches had the Church Army taking much of the services, and Dennis preached good, challenging sermons. Holiday Guides added to the Ennerdale congregation, and Dennis got them involved in activities which they seemed to enjoy. On Monday the team visited homes in

Ennerdale and managed to persuade fifty children to come to an early evening party. It was an energetic time for the team who then slowed down the activity with stories with a Christian message and some good songs. The team returned to us for supper feeling flat out.

Kirkland was well visited on Tuesday and they went to lunch with parishioners, the Rutherfords, who were keen church workers. The team felt they had a rewarding day, especially in the evening in the home of Joyce Litt where some of the Kirkland folk were invited to meet the team. We had a good attendance at the Wednesday HC and some of the mums and babes and two grannies came back to the Vicarage for coffee. Mrs. Rickerby had invited the team to lunch. In the evening we had quite a crowd in for coffee and a talk by the team. Sara, Jonathan and Helen on the team led some hymn singing accompanying them with violin and guitars. This went down well and the company were reluctant to leave for home.

We had to part with this cheerful company the next day, but took the team down to the lake for a short walk, we then left them finishing off visits to Lamplugh homes. On our return to the Vicarage one could still hear the echo of their cheerful banter. We had enjoyed talks with them, and there is always that feeling of being one family when we find we are all on the same spiritual wavelength. We hoped their paths and ours might cross again sometime. All seemed to feel refreshed by their preaching and teaching and sharing of experiences in the Christian faith.

While Elisabeth was away in Scotland helping Gordon with a choir Camp, Sara was kept busy helping John and Mary to get the hay in, as rain threatened, and they were pleased to get at least forty really dry bales under cover. I was busy on the domestic scene getting spare rooms ready for any future invasion. Raymond was at a meeting in Lamplugh and George Sixsmith rang to say he was coming the next day to attend to all three organs. Kirkland organ was given a new blower, so no more hand pumping.

That evening, who should turn up but Peter Brown, our former curate at Faringdon, with Meg, and their four children and Toby the dog. They parked their caravan on our drive and had an evening meal with us. Ennerdale had a united service so we had a full church including a baptism party. Some new neighbours of the Hill family came with the Hills to coffee at the Vicarage after service, and the Browns joined us for lunch, Sara then went to the Mitchells after we had walked the dogs, and I got tea for the Browns. Raymond, Peter and I went to church in Whitehaven and the Vicar, Alan Postlethwaite, preached an excellent sermon on the Holy Spirit. It was good to see Alan again. He had been an ordinand from Barrow and we knew him and his family. (He once drove a steam train on an excursion to York that we went on, and happily all went well!) Lyn Hill and Sara entertained the Browns the next day, taking the four Brown children and the three Hill girls to Cosra Moss, and they walked by the lake also.

Elisabeth rang from Manchester asking Dad if he could collect her from Manchester the next day as she was now leaving and had a lot of stuff to bring home as she was clearing her flat. Raymond was off the next morning at 6.30am and had a very long day helping Liz and they were grateful to Chris Lloyd giving them lunch. They set off for Ennerdale at 6.30 in the evening and were worried in Keswick to find the car tyres ballooning with the weight. A garage advised them to drive home slowly and the tyre was not likely to burst. They did make it without mishap but were relieved to get home at 10.30pm. Sara, Peter and Meg did most of the unloading of the roof and interior of the car and helped to get it all stacked in Elisabeth's room.

It took Elisabeth some days to get sorted out and was hardly ready when a college friend, Sandra, turned up for a week's holiday. I was glad of their help with dog walking, but I was very concerned for Topsy whom I kept at home as she was losing ground and obviously would not live much longer, but the vet was keeping her going with injections. He agreed with me that she was not ready to leave us yet, and obviously did not want to be parted from Snoopy, her nine year-old pup. It saddened me greatly to see Topsy failing. She was a wonderful Jack Russell and had provided us with great joy with the twenty pups she and Towser had had in four litters; Snoopy was retained as her last pup. Topsy still would patiently wash Snoopy all over if he came in wet from a walk, still her baby. It was a joy to us to have Elisabeth and Sara home until the end of September. We were all kept busy with parish activities, and Sara was helping at the Mitchell's farm quite often, while Elisabeth had lots of friends coming on visits. On 24 September Raymond drove off to take the girls and much luggage to their respective teacher training colleges. It was a depressing day on my own but I had plenty of work to pass the hours until Raymond's return cheered me. The girls had settled happily into their new surroundings.

We were glad to hear Cara and Jill were coming up for a week. Raymond had a busy week of engagements so did not get outings with Cara and Jill but I took a week off from church activity to get out and about with them when I could.

Though the harvest had not been easy owing to much interruption by rain, we had the usual cheering Harvest Festival services.

From Autumn into Winter 1979

We had two Harvest Festivals as Raymond was invited back to St. Paul's, Barrow to preach at Evensong at their Harvest Festival. It was a great joy to be back in that church amongst our old family, and Raymond got such a loving reception. Though no Margaret Taylor, two of her choirmen were still in the choir, and to see them singing away as of old brought tears to my eyes, remembering the wonderful choir and music of Margaret's day. I saw Mrs. Beach wiping her eyes as Raymond descended from the pulpit and I could see she also was living in that great past. Such happy days that we would ever be grateful to God for having led us to St. Paul's.

My War Ag. colleague of Land Army days, Ursula Yates, came and spent a week with us, and it was good to be walking dogs with her once more. We were lucky to have lovely weather for her to see autumn at its best.

Congregations were small even for Ennerdale and Lamplugh with plenty of work still on the farms. Looking at the twelve in Ennerdale and the few in Kirkland, I found myself reflecting again on the 250 the previous week in Barrow. However it was our pre-retirement parish and a very happy family, and we understood our parishioners were very hard at work on Sundays as other days. Raymond was encouraged by gathering a good lot of Confirmation candidates again, and I enjoyed having them in for tea before their session with Raymond. It saddened us to have a message from St. Paul's Vicar, Frank Dean to tell us of the death of dear Miss Butler, who had taken us on those wonderful holidays at Portmerion with the children and dogs. We were sad not to be able to attend her funeral, especially as Frank told us very few attended. Raymond and I had enjoyable visits to all the homes of the Confirmation candidates.

We had an enjoyable visit from the Bishop of Penrith, who dropped in to have tea with us towards the end of November. We raised the subject of retirement and the Bishop said he would make some enquiries about possible retirement homes. He thought the Diocese and Church commissioners would be the people to approach. We were pleasantly surprised by a good congregation despite a very wet evening. All but two of the Confirmation class came to church and to the Vicarage afterwards.

The next day we had Lyn Oliver from Faringdon and her guide dog to meet quite late in Cockermouth. Lyn had an idea she would like to live in Cumbria. She visited Cockermouth but prices were a bit beyond her. While Lyn walked dogs I got busy on Christmas fare, making cakes and puddings. We still had a lot of youngsters coming to the mid-week communion with their Mums. This was always an enjoyable session and the mums enjoyed having adult company for the morning. On our day off I managed to sell some of the Great Britain stamp collection I had worked on for some years and we decided to get a good radio cassette recorder to enjoy in our retirement.

Sara got home from college early in December, and Elisabeth also was to be met in Carlisle a few days later. Raymond and I were early into Carlisle, and we each went to our respective hairdressers and decided to meet at the station to collect Elisabeth. I waited around and suddenly saw a note under the windscreen wiper. It was from the police informing me that Raymond had collapsed in the street and had been taken to hospital. Elisabeth arrived as I was reading this and immediately rang the Police to enquire which hospital and how to get there. I had a spare car key so Liz took the wheel and guided us safely through the Christmas crowds and traffic. I was thankful Elisabeth was a good driver and got us quite quickly to the hospital.

It was such a relief to Liz and me to find Raymond sitting up on a hospital trolley, with a group of attractive young nurses giving him tea. Clearly the 'James Mason' look was not lost on them. He was getting spoilt and quite enjoying the attention. The Doctor said he had evidently fainted coming out of a hot store to the very bleak weather. He suggested Elisabeth should the drive us back to Ennerdale, which she was quite happy to do. When I suggested to Raymond he would be wise to retire before weathering another Northern winter, though it was an unwelcome thought to have to retire before he was seventy, he realised his health was failing.

Sara delayed coming home in the Christmas holiday to have a skiing holiday in Italy and, when she returned, was happy to have won a gold badge in skiing tests. We saw the New Year in together and then the girls were off to college at the beginning of January.

There was no snow yet but lashings of rain made life a bit dismal without the girls at home, and our postman Harry said driving conditions were making travel difficult on his rounds.

As we settled back to routine, Raymond felt he had now better let the Bishop know that he felt he should retire this year, though sad to leave Ennerdale. It was not an easy decision but he thought the parish now deserved a younger Vicar. Where, we wondered, would we be spending next Christmas and New Year?

Approaching Retirement

••

The big interest in Ennerdale that Spring of 1980 was the worry of Windscale wanting to take over Ennerdale Water and Wastwater to wash nuclear waste, two lakes that offered the purest water. There was tremendous opposition to this proposal and a long drawn out series of meetings to hear the public's views. Raymond wrote to many M.P.s to protest and also wrote to members of the Royal Family. Anxiety grew when work was started round the lake before the matter was decided. It was with great relief when, after some months, Windscale was not given permission to use these beautiful lakes.

Sara and Elisabeth both did a fair bit of organ playing for the services at Lamplugh and Ennerdale, and Sara was sometimes roped in for piano-playing for children's parties. All too soon both were off to finish their teacher training. They were lucky with applications to teach in private schools. Elisabeth was appointed head of music in a boys' prep school – Lathallen School, near Montrose. The school building was a castle near the sea. Sara was appointed to a school Terra Nova, near Manchester. Both were pleased to have something fixed before Dad retired, as many teachers were having difficulty in getting jobs at the time.

We were cheered by quite an increase in attendance at church, and more young families and older folk were coming to the Wednesday services, and joining us for coffee after.

I was very sad when my beloved Jack Russell Topsy, was obviously at the end of her tether, and I had to ask the vet to come and put her to sleep. The Vet was sad to have to give Topsy her fatal injection as he loved Jack Russells and had had one very like Topsy, also a good footballer. I nursed Topsy while she had the injection and she licked the arm of the vet as he put the needle in. While he carried her little form away to his van I made a coffee for us both and we talked cheerfully about everything except dogs. The girls both rang up to say how sad they were to get my letter with the news and were glad they were not home to see her go.

I walked Snoopy and Jet in John and Mary's fields and, though they were in the next field digging, I couldn't face them with the news of Topsy's departure. As it happened they were burying a greatly loved sheepdog who had died with some internal injury, so I suppose we could have wept together. They were as soft about dogs as I was. Sara was home for a weekend in February and was roped in to help with the Sunday School. She then baked herself cakes and biscuits to take back to college and was off again very early on Tuesday. Snow was being driven on gales so I was glad to hear she had arrived safely.

The Bishop wrote to Raymond about a date for his retirement and told him what money was available from the Diocese and the Church Commissioners for a retirement home. We realised we ought to be giving this serious consideration and should look around at houses. As it is not thought right to retire too near one's parish we were a bit at a loss to decide where to live, and we had so little time to go house hunting. We looked around a few homes in Whitehaven and Cockermouth, but not within our price limit. We also felt that would be considered too near Ennerdale. It is not considered kind to the next incumbent to settle on their doorstep. It is always a temptation to some ex-parishioners to drive over to their former Vicar's church, and this is not helpful to the new Vicar's confidence.

The Ash Wednesday services were really well attended and up to ten adults and eight children came to the Vicarage for refreshments and these encouraging numbers kept up during Lent. This made the thought of retirement less attractive but I felt it would not be wise to stay for another winter.

The Bishop of Penrith told Raymond he would do what he could to help with the problem of finding a retirement home. He was sad however that it was ill-health that was influencing Raymond's reluctant decision that he ought to retire though the local retired clergy did tell Raymond he could count on them for any help that might be needed.

In March I became an old-age pensioner, though Raymond could have already been claiming his state pension. We decided not to claim it until we were actually retired. This meant we would benefit from an increase in pension in retirement. Elisabeth and Sara were home for Easter and both were roped in to do some organ playing for some of the services. John Mitchell also kept Sara entertained, helping him with dipping over a hundred sheep.

On Easter Monday, after very enjoyable services with good numbers at all the churches, we had an invasion of the Hancock family – John and Margaret and the four children as well as Hilda and Horace Hayhurst who came to stay for a few days. I was not too disappointed when Chris Lloyd rang to say she could not, after all, manage a visit that week. Twelve for meals were fun enough. Mrs. Hayhurst and Margaret were very helpful, and they managed quite a lot of outings in Ennerdale area, and we were able to join in some. Horace knew so many great walks and had climbed most of the heights. When they had returned to work, Evelyn Campbell paid us a visit, and I was glad of her company while Raymond was at a Diocesan Meeting.

Raymond was pleased to receive very kind letters about the Good Friday three-hour Service he had taken at a Maryport church. It had been a wonderful three hours because the congregation built up every quarter of an hour, and very few left at these times. There was a well filled church by the end of the service. I felt we were as the New Testament puts it, all in once place and of one mind. The atmosphere was inspired and Raymond's addresses included much teaching from the old and new testament, showing the relevance of the one to the other. These letters Raymond received told of some staying the full three hours for the first time, and the time had felt much shorter. One asked if he could have a copy of the sermons.

Raymond was unable to do so, as he only had notes. When the listening was so intense there was so inspired an atmosphere that Raymond said he was unable to remember what was said. With so attentive a listening the Holy Spirit takes over. It was one of the most inspired services I had attended and the church seemed to light up and there was the very real feeling of the Heavenly Host present with us. It was the last three-hour service taken by Raymond. I was so thankful I was able to be with him in Maryport that special day.

To Be or Not To Be the South Coast

● ●

A letter from the C. of E. Pensions Board told us that a very pleasant house had been willed to them by a Clergyman who had no relatives needing it and was available for us if we cared to move to Seaford in Sussex. They would like a quick decision on this as they did not want it to stay empty for long. This was on 12th May and we really could not manage to visit Seaford for about three weeks, but would quickly decide once we saw the property.

Raymond was trying to get permission for a memorial plate to be fixed in Lamplugh Church. It was a memorial to little Tamlyn Dickenson, the first grandson of Ronald and Pam Dickenson. Ronald's son had moved to Australia and, while staying in a high flat with his wife's mother until they found their own home, Tamlyn crawled out of the flat and fell through railings to the ground floor and was killed instantly. Not only were Ron and Pam and Tamlyn's parents quite devastated, but all Lamplugh. Tamlyn was living with Granny and Grandad Dickenson in Lamplugh immediately before their departure to Australia so was known to many as a lovely babe. Tamlyn's Dad had had his misery eased somewhat after having a very wonderful vision of little Tamlyn playing very happily in heaven. The 'powers that be' did not approve of having 'Playing happily in Heaven' engraved on a brass plate. However, as the church had so many Dickenson memorials, Raymond managed to get permission and the memorial was shortly to be blessed in a little service. A lot of people attended the service which was a comfort to many.

Raymond had also agreed to look at a Parish in the New Forest which wanted an assistant retired priest in exchange for a cottage to live in. This was turned down as it was to be a lot of work and little income. We decided to waste no more time but to look at what Seaford had to offer.

Evelyn was to have a few more days with us. We took her to Whitehaven as we were doing a round of the shops and who should we meet but our last curate of Barrow days, now an Army chaplain,

Peter Mosley, his wife Sheelagh and their daughters Hilary and Nicola, and they all returned to Ennerdale for lunch with us. The daughters were at school in Cumbria. Peter was very happy in the Army chaplaincy, but I had a feeling Sheelagh's feelings about life with Army wives were a bit mixed. The girls were hardly recognisable as we had last seen them as babes. We had a few last outings with Evelyn, and she was pleased to note we had rather more people coming to coffee on Wednesdays and enjoyed the children playing together. On her last evening with us Evelyn joined our weekly prayer group and enjoyed the discussions and company.

It was May before we visited Seaford. We went to Bournemouth for a night and Cara drove us over to Sussex. Cara had done Child Officer work in East Sussex so was familiar with Seaford, having visited Children's Homes there. One quick look at the house on a very pleasant quiet road, yet near shops, the sea, and beautiful downland, and the house having a large pleasant garden, we decided to ring the Pension Board right away to say we would be delighted to accept the use of 3 Tudor Close.

After a snack lunch in town we returned to the house to do some measuring of rooms and windows. After calling on Raymond's brother and his wife, Bernard and Margaret, living in Washington, West Sussex, we eventually got to Bournemouth at 8pm. Jill had supper ready so we ate with them and then Cara took us to Aunt Grett for our two nights with her. After a quiet day of pottering round shops in Southbourne with Aunt Grett, we settled for an early night having arranged with the Haleys in Barrow to drive us to Ennerdale from Whitehaven station and to spend two nights with us in Ennerdale.

Raymond wrote to the Bishop about retirement the day after our return. It was decided that August would be a good time to leave the parish when the Parishes had got the summer events over, and a pleasant time of year for a removal. When this was suggested to the Pension Board, they were keen for our removal to take place in June. After some thought we decided that Tudor Croft being so small, we surely had enough furniture to furnish it, and yet leave enough in the Vicarage to live there for two months or so. We told the Pension Board we would furnish Tudor Croft in June, and pay maintenance from that date, but could not move until the parish summer events were over. They were very understanding and agreed to that. Our feelings were mixed, and Raymond felt sad when he had to send back to the Bishop his licence as a Diocesan Priest. After forty-three years in the Ministry he found it hard to think of life without his own parish in future.

From then on we were busy thinking what furniture we would be able to take to Seaford. We quite often went to a furniture shop in Keswick where they bought and sold second-hand furniture as well as new. The sales went well and we felt it would be helpful to earn some money to buy curtains and carpets for Seaford. These outings were on days off; the rest of the time life was pretty frantic. Not only visitors and family wanting to see Ennerdale before we left, but lots of invitations out to friends, once they were told we were to leave Ennerdale in August. There was of course the Ennerdale Show, and there were sales of work at all the churches. Raymond had a Confirmation class to prepare and the Confirmation service to arrange, and there were weddings to which we were invited. A very busy summer.

The judging of the Herdwick sheep: Ennerdale Show.

June 1st was Trinity Sunday and the forty-second anniversary of Raymond's Ordination to the Priesthood. Raymond decided to announce he was to retire in August. This would allow the Church to begin finding a successor, hopefully without too long an interregnum.

Ennerdale seemed to take the news in its stride, but one young man, a recent arrival in Ennerdale, wished us a happy retirement. One at Kirkland also wished Raymond well. At Lamplugh one lady said to Raymond that his announcement had ruined her day, while another said it had come as a bombshell. On the whole, however, no one seemed too surprised nor sad. The Evening Service was a Youth Service and youngsters from Hensingham came as a witness team and were well received, and the Confirmation class was appreciative of their chat after Service.

Cara, Jill and Flo' arrived for a holiday. The visitors were out and about much of their stay. They visited Carlisle one day and Scotland the next day before spending time in the more local towns. The Jaimiesons had been away so we went to see them and they were very sad to hear Raymond was leaving. We had phone calls from the Hockings and the Rickerbys saying how very sad they were to hear the news. We felt that we were probably a lot more sad than the parishes. It had been such a joy to return up north and we found it hard to believe it would be as easy to make new friends on the south coast. Every day we tried to get some sorting and packing done if we had free

Raymond visits Jim & Hilda Rickerby at their farm near Ennerdale.

hours. The family helped too in the evenings. A gentleman came to look through books Raymond decided to sell and Raymond was pleased with a cheque for £56 and Elisabeth managed to sell music books too and was happy to have £37 for books she no longer required.

The Seaford Die Cast

Tom Roper was really sad when signing as witness to Raymond's resignation form for the Bishop of Carlisle. Tom was a bit worried about whether they would get another Vicar as there had been a long interregnum before Raymond accepted the living. The Archdeacon was going to see the parishes and would be meeting the PCC.

On 8th June the Confirmation Service in Lamplugh drew so large a congregation that some were crammed with the choir in their stalls. There were 98 communicants. The Wednesday services were becoming ever better attended by more adults and more toddlers. Twelve adults and nine or ten young children was quite usual. I was clearing the dining room, so a friend in the village in the Forestry cottages took over the drinks and biscuit meeting after services. These were very happy occasions we were going to miss.

The Bibbys retrieved their donkeys from the front paddock at the Vicarage; they hadn't sufficient grass as the weather had been so dry. Snoopy missed them as he loved to jump the fence and enjoyed being chased by the donkeys. When he'd had enough he sailed over the fence to the intense frustration of the donkeys. The front paddock looked very bare without them.

Our Barrow firm of furniture removers was to come at the beginning of July but in fact didn't manage to come until 4th August. From June onwards life was really frantic. Sara and Elisabeth both left their teacher training schools, so we had travels to them to get all their clutter safely home and they had a busy time ahead sorting, discarding, selling and bundling up things for charity shops. We were labelling which furniture was bound for Seaford, and which was to be disposed of locally. At the same time there was a need of more visiting; we entertained friends to meals and were ourselves getting lots of farewell invitations out.

The Morning Service on Wednesday, 2nd July was followed as usual by the gathering for coffee, now at the Forestry cottage, and Joy providing the drinks and biscuits. The weather was perfect for a garden meeting and we were six Mums and eight children, all playing happily while we reminisced a bit about all our happy gatherings.

Elisabeth had gone early to Heversham Church where our former Barrow curate, John Hancock, was Vicar and had persuaded Elisabeth to give an organ recital that evening. We were to travel later after the dogs had been well exercised as we might return home rather late. Sara took the dogs out and urged us to set off in good time as she was to be page turner for Elisabeth. John Hancock had said he would take a tape recording of the recital, and he helped another gentleman to fix up his tape recorder, so we were given copies.

There was a good attendance and all seemed pleased with an evening of fairly well known classical works. Though nervous, Sara managed her part successfully and both got a lot of applause at the end. Some joined us all for refreshments after the recital. John was pleased with the evening. He told us some time later that he had a visit from a friend who was organist of Lichfield Cathedral. When listening to the recording of the recital John was asked, 'Is that a Gillian Weir recording?" John told him it was one of her pupils, and this did not surprise him.

In mid-July we had a brief visit to Bournemouth and visited Seaford to let the girls see our new home and to try to assess what furniture would fit in and to imagine how all should be arranged.

Nearer and Nearer Comes the Time

I decided I must travel to Bournemouth on Friday 1st August when we had a call from our Barrow Furniture remover, Ken Surphlis, to say he would collect furniture for Seaford on Monday, and it would be unloaded in Seaford on Tuesday 6th. My sister Cara said she would drive us over to Seaford on 5th to get ready for the furniture arrival. The day before I set off for Bournemouth we had a visit from Barrow friends, Nicholas Spencer and his father, Richard. Nicholas was one of the three Spencer sons who had been at the St. Paul's Junior school with Elisabeth and Sara. He happened to be on a week's annual leave from the Benedictine Monastery as he had become a monk in his early twenties. It was interesting to hear about his new life and his enjoyment of being employed in the garden much of his time. He was thoroughly happy but a bit sad he saw little of his brothers now. His parents were able to visit him at certain times and he kept in touch with all by post. His brothers were married and had children. Elisabeth and Sara enjoyed some reminiscing with Nick about their St. Paul's school days. It was good of Nick to spare a day of his brief week to visit us while he was in Barrow.

Elisabeth and Sara accompanied me to Carlisle Station. I had a good train journey with only a change in Birmingham and found Cara waiting with the car at Bournemouth station. We had a quiet Saturday and Sunday, having shopped on Saturday, gathering things we thought would be useful in the empty Seaford house, waiting for the furniture. Raymond rang up in the evening to say Ken Surphlis had been with the removal men, to see that all went well, and making sure the valuable Bosendorfer piano was packed and handled well. Ennerdale Vicarage was looking pretty bare. Elisabeth and Sara had been busy tidying after the men left.

Cara and I decided on a quiet Sunday. We went to early service and left Jill coping with preparations for a roast beef lunch, as Brother Bill was coming to join us. She was also building up our strength for removal day. We made an early start the next morning, having loaded up the necessities for the next day before retiring to bed. We would have time for some shopping in Seaford as the removers were not arriving until early Tuesday morning. As soon as we arrived Cara went to buy paints to do the walls of the sitting room and the main bedroom. I spent time trying to fix curtain wires. We also remembered to buy electric light pulls for all the rooms, so we were well occupied.

The evening passed quickly as we did a lot of phoning, Cara in touch with Jill and I had a long session with Ennerdale. Sara said they had had a pretty wet day for the loading of the furniture, but the men worked well and speedily with the boss directing operations. Sara said the house looked rather lovely with so many empty rooms. The kitchen still had adequate necessities and, even if the day of the Ennerdale sale to be held in Vicarage grounds happened to be wet, they would have room for the sale indoors. This sale and garden party was to be on 16th Saturday, so I would have time to prepare for it as I would be home the Saturday before. Sara told me that the Simpsons hoped to see us again soon as they were coming over to meet the PCC. We would be able to be at the Ennerdale Show just three days before Raymond's final Sunday, which would be his retirement day.

Cara and I settled on our camp beds on bare floors quite early but neither of us had a very good night. I was still mentally arranging furniture! The Ken Surphlis van arrived around 9am. The men set to work at once, bringing in all the carpets for a start, and not waiting for us to roll out the underfelts were rapidly filling the house with the furniture. They got lots of it in the right place, but were slow bringing in the many cartons I had carefully labelled with the room numbers. It came as a surprise at around noon when they told us all was now unloaded and they were off to have a picnic on the beach with their wives as it was such a nice day. They said we'd find some things in the garage. It seems there was one Ken Surphlis man who had driven the van down, the other men were hired locally. With some dismay we found the garage almost filled to the roof with all the well labelled cartons.

Elisabeth had volunteered to help sort out the house before we left Ennerdale; she was accompanying Gordon to Sussex as he had a Recital not far from Seaford. Cara and I felt we must try to get the kitchen and bedrooms somewhat organised. We worked till quite late until satisfied the kitchen and the three bedrooms supplied with necessities.

Cara had told me they were expecting a visit from Lizzie Burford, who had been Mother's help when we were all babes, living in Tredegar. Lizzie and her daughter Mary were to be on a coach outing and Lizzie so wanted to see the three of us and brother Bill if possible, as we'd not met for many years. We had to be up in good time though feeling the effects of our late night.

Lizzie and Mary arrived in time for a light lunch and we had time to take them to Bill's house before they had to return to the coach. Lizzie had brought us each a brass model of miners' lamps which were musical boxes and played 'Land of my Fathers'. Since we were all born in Tredegar, we could well remember the sound of the miners' clogs coming past our house early morning. Their faces black, their hats with the lamp at the front, and the miners were often singing, talking and laughing. We were not to talk until after we'd heard the morning hooter from the mines when the shifts changed, but Bill was awake earlier most days and used to try to make a hooter noise so that he could wake us up to play. We enjoyed the reminiscing with Lizzie and were only sad that mother and her miner husband had now both died. Lizzie would so have loved to see mother again, and felt pretty lost without Albert.

The return journey to Ennerdale meant a change at Barrow, and then a train to Whitehaven where Raymond met me. I was back in time to be a guest at the wedding of Linda Rickerby. I became sidesman as there was no one to hand out service sheets, and there was a lovely full church and a joyful service.

Sara was then off to a Beach Mission in which the school took part. We heard that the Simpsons, having accepted the living, would be over on 17th August to meet the PCC and would drop in to tea with us. The day before we were having a Vicarage garden party and sale of work in the garden. Fortunately it was a lovely day after a rather wet start. The opener was Tommy Thomas from Radio Carlisle, and he seemed to draw the crowds as the sale was well attended – maybe as it was our last sale that encouraged good attendance.

We greatly enjoyed the visit of Peter and Barbara Simpson and were very pleased they hoped to announce their acceptance of the parish before we left. It would reassure those who were afraid they might not get another Vicar but be attached to other churches to share their Vicar. We promised them we would be up sometime to visit Ennerdale and would call on them to see how they were enjoying country life. They were interested to hear Ennerdale Vicarage had had their garden party and sale the day before, and they wished they had known and could have dropped in. There was a splendid attendance and a very happy spirit prevailed; we got lots of good wishes for our retirement. The Sale raised £209 which they thought a good achievement as it was considered to be more of a party and a final meeting with us than a sale.

Our last week passed quickly with many folk looking in to say farewell. Cousin Alan and Betty came over from Silecroft to have lunch with us. They said it seemed only a short time since they came to help us move in and were quite sorry we were to go quite so far away. On Saturday we went to Keswick and Sara met up with a school friend. We returned via Newlands Valley to enjoy the mountain and lake views.

Raymond, having taken his last services at Lamplugh and Kirkland on Sunday on Monday, the next day drove Elisabeth to Montrose. They spent a night as guests of the Headmaster, and his wife, Mr. and Mrs. de Jonse. Elisabeth also met the Vicar of her church in Montrose where she was to be appointed organist. She was pleased to find it a very impressive organ. Elisabeth left her books at the school, returned home with Raymond and shared the driving. Sara was helping John and Mary Mitchell with the haymaking and, despite a fairly empty house, I found lots there to occupy me.

Farewells

• •

Ennerdale Show was on Wednesday but we had the Haleys visiting, from Barrow and four came to coffee after the usual Wednesday Service and only Sue brought her babies. There were eight adults at the Service which was nice for our final Wednesday. After an early lunch with the Haleys we all made for the show and enjoyed wandering round for several hours. Gladys and Herbert returned to the Vicarage with us for tea and then left for Barrow at about 5.30pm. In the evening Mable Proctor had a study and prayer group and we joined the six there for a final get together. It went on quite late and we eventually got to bed at midnight.

On Friday we visited friends in Barrow and did some shopping and in the evening went out to supper with friends. Saturday morning found us seeing friends in Cockermouth and Keswick, and returned home to have an unexpected visit from the Vicar of Windermere, Ted Barker and his wife, who had been at a Barrow church when we were at St. Paul's. They had come to wish us a happy retirement.

Knowing how sad Raymond felt at having to give the Blessing on Sunday for the last time to his own church family, I had written to friends of all our former parishes together, asking for prayers on our final Sunday, 31st August. Ted and Elaine Barker assured us that their prayers would certainly be with us on Sunday. We spent almost all Saturday evening receiving phone calls from so many friends from all over, and we were delighted to have quite a long chat with Richard Hare, Bishop of Pontefract, who was a friend of our Barrow days. He knew Seaford well and assured us we would love it and the lovely Sussex downland. After so many calls we were really feeling this was all quite unreal. Richard Hare's assurance that we were to be happy in Seaford was helpful. I felt sure this move was arranged by God so we really had nothing to fear. It was consoling that the parting would now soon be over.

It was pleasant to have the distraction of a visit from the Haleys around 9.30 am when I had walked the dogs, and the girls were

Walking the dogs on the Mitchells' Farm.

Down the long drive from Ennerdale Vicarage.so beautifully adorned with daffodils in sporing.

more or less packed up to go to Manchester. Sara was off to Terra Nova school, but was staying with Elisabeth at Gordon's home for a day or two on her way to Terra Nova, and Elisabeth would travel up to Montrose soon after. The Haleys went to Ennerdale church around 10am. I went just before 10.30am. It was nice to have the Haleys to represent Barrow congregation, and to my astonishment I saw Valerie and Peter Hannaway, Faringdon friends, in church. Just as the service began, in bustled Rhoda Booth and her sister. Rhoda lived in Bradford and had been a social work assistant in my almoner department. She had been at our Bradford Cathedral wedding and had paid visits to us in Hildenborough but we had not met for some years. She said that when she heard Raymond was retiring that she must be there to support us on our last Sunday. She had set off from Bradford early and just made it to the service.

I had had phone calls from Hildenborough telling us we would be much in their thoughts and it was a wonderful way to finish Vicarage days to have so many of our church 'families' with us in spirit on this occasion. After service we were invited up to Kirkland for the official farewell. In Kirkland there was a wonderful buffet lunch awaiting us and a great gathering from all the churches. A joyful feast, but sadness was to the fore as we took our farewells, though we were not leaving the Vicarage until Tuesday as there was the final clearing up to do.

The Haleys walked our dogs for us before they left. Elisabeth and Sara left us around 3pm and telephoned us from Gordon's to let us know they had arrived safely. Raymond and I settled around 1am after achieving a bit more packing. As 1st September dawned, we did a final clearance of our lovely Vicarage, though Monica Simpson, our Roman Catholic friend who so often attended our churches, had been in the previous day sweeping all the empty rooms and doing all she could to help. Monica assured us she would be down south before long to visit us and to see us in our new surroundings as she visited London from time to time.

With heavy heart I took the dogs a last walk in the Mitchells' farm and left Jet with Mary. My vet had advised against taking Jet away from the country to a town as he was fourteen years-old and his hind legs were showing his age. He suggested it would be kinder to have him put to sleep. John Mitchell said he would not let Jet be put to sleep and he could join his twelve collie bitches to live out his life. He joined Mary and set off with her to find John in the fields and didn't give Snoopy and me a second look. Snoopy was very reluctant to leave Jet, but I couldn't part with Snoopy, and I would find him a new companion as soon as we got to Seaford. (That proved very easy as Elisabeth wrote asking us to look after her Westie; Lucy and Snoopy fell in love at first sight and they were great pals.)

Just before we set off down our long drive for the last time, Ronald and Pam Dickenson came to say farewell and to give us the good news that they had just heard they had another grandson in Australia. They were off soon to visit the family. Ron said that on his return to Lamplugh he would do us a painting of Ennerdale and would hope we would return to collect it. He would invite parishioners to come and attend the presentation. This was a very happy prospect as we could think of no better souvenir of our happy Ennerdale days.

On our way out of the Parish we called on Tom and Marjorie Jaimeson. Tom had a copy of Raymond's last magazine for us, and they hoped to see us before long as we had said we would be up to collect a painting by Ron Dickenson that he hoped to have painted by next year, when they returned from their visit to Australia.

As we left Cumbria and got on to the motorways we both felt tiredness was taking over and we had plenty to reflect on as we looked back over our Vicarage years. For Raymond it was a case of remembering his ordinations in Southwark Cathedral when I was 16-17 years-old. I often so wished we could have known one another then, in 1937, but we each had our war to deal with. While I was helping to keep the Nation fed, Raymond was keeping up the spirits of the servicemen in North Africa, travelling many miles from camp to camp in the desert. I felt God must have meant us to meet as I was accepted on a post-graduate course of training as a hospital almoner, though I hadn't even a school certificate, let alone a degree. The course did not have exams, just continual assessment, so I did become a professional medical social worker. I soon found at hospital interviews that most applicants were so much better qualified, it was not likely I'd get a job. At one interview I was interested to hear the other applicants saying that Bradford Hospital was most unlikely to get more almoners. It was a most unattractive place to work. I went straight off home to apply for a job in Bradford and got it as the only applicant, and in my first week in Bradford attended the Cathedral, and there was Raymond. What a wonderful life had then opened for me. How the great sadness of losing our first two babes was compensated by the two lovely daughters we had, and how Hildenborough had rejoiced with us.

Never would the glow of joy of our days in Barrow fade and that great day when the completion of the building of St. Paul's Church brought Bishop Bulley, then Bishop of Carlisle, to consecrate the completed church. How the church had fairly rocked to the joyful singing of that great choir and vast congregation – such a wonderful atmosphere of jubilation.

It certainly took us time to adjust to the smaller, very different town of Faringdon. Though quite quickly aware that there were those not impressed with Raymond's ministry, we made a lot of good friends whose ready cooperation in bringing a brighter look to the church and giving support to Raymond was a great encouragement. When discontent with Raymond's ministry became more pronounced and we were becoming more conscious of our advancing years, the offer of a move to Lamplugh with Ennerdale in Cumbria proved to be the perfect 'swansong' parish to bring Raymond's days as a Vicar to a happy end.

Mulling over these memories while travelling south, a sense of serenity, peace and gratitude to God took over, and that lovely hymn of praise came to mind so aptly expressing how I now felt:

When all Thy mercies O my God, my rising soul surveys, transported with the view I'm lost in wonder love and Praise.

Raymond and Anne Fountain, with Snoopy and Susie
outside Tudor Croft, Seaford.

POSTSCRIPT

Settling in Seaford was much easier than expected because we not only got a great welcome from the local clergy, but found ourselves surrounded by welcoming kindly neighbours. We were soon able to pop into one another's homes as if we'd always been neighbours. The Vicar of St. Leonard's Church in the town was quick to invite Raymond to assist him in the Church and Deanery. Canon Williams, who helped Michael Thompson, was also retired but doing a lot of work with Michael. Raymond soon felt at home in the churches locally and found great enjoyment in still being able to take services and preach, without the other parish duties.

For six years we greatly enjoyed the freedom of retirement and made many friends. I particularly enjoyed having Raymond sitting with me in church, which one cannot enjoy very much in the Vicarage years. Sadly, Raymond's earthly ministry ended in December 1986, when he died on St. Stephen's Day, 26th December, after a severe coronary heart attack.

A year later Elisabeth married a student she met at Lincoln Theological College. In June 1988 I attended the service in Coventry Cathedral when my son in law Ronald was ordained Priest, and Elisabeth was ordained Deacon. In November that year the safe arrival of their son, James made me a very happy grandmother, and James was followed by the birth of young brother Michael in March 1991, giving me much joy.

In October 1993 my younger daughter, Sara, married a librarian colleague, Peter Sage. Their wedding at St. Leonard's Church, Seaford, was taken by the Vicar, Michael Thompson. A lovely service in a full church, though Michael was then critically ill with cancer. Those who did not know Michael did not realise that he was critically ill, he took the service so cheerily and well. It was the last service he was able to take.

Sara and Peter live quite near me in Seaford, and they and their young son, Adam, and his young sister, Catherine, greatly enrich life in Seaford for me. So all:

Praise to the Holiest in the height
And in the depth be praise,
In all His words most wonderful,
Most sure in all His ways.

More books from Ex Libris Press:

LAND GIRL: *Her story of six years in the Women's Land Army, 1940-46* by Anne Hall
Our perennial bestseller
144 pages; Illustrated
Price £4.95

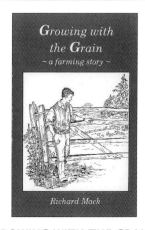

GROWING WITH THE GRAIN: *A farming story* by Richard Mack
Hugely entertaining!
160 pages; Illustrated
Price £4.95

GRAN'S OLD-FASHIONED REMEDIES, WRINKLES AND RECIPES by Jean Penny
'A most useful and delightful book.'
96 pages; Illustrated
Price £3.50

GRAN'S OLD-FASHIONED GARDENING GEMS
by Jean Penny
Packed full of tips aimed at the reluctant gardener.
96 pages; Illustrated
Price £3.50